Yellow Mountain

May Lin de Chezelles

Clink
Street

Published by Clink Street Publishing 2022

Copyright © 2022

First edition.

ISBN:
978-1-915229-25-0 - paperback
978-1-915229-26-7 - ebook

JML de Cheyeller

Prologue

Yellow Mountain is written as a piece of biographical fiction. Adapted from the translated (Chinese) diaries of my mother, it gives an account of the migration of her family from China to Malaya as it was then known. It is a patchwork quilt of stories told to her by her father. These accounts show the inimitable father-daughter relationship which developed during the journey and the remarkable way in which he rebuilt his life in a country quite unlike his own. He is buried next to his wife in the Christian Cemetery, in Taiping, Malaysia.

To Simon .... *whose love make life brighter*

To Susan .... *my eternally dazzling mother*

To William .... *a good communicator to the Chinese people*
and who makes me laugh

CHAPTER ONE

Huangsan

Conversations can sometimes be so prolific in the sense that they span time, history and cultures. I had many such conversations with my mother. Additionally, between us I often felt that there was an invisible red silk thread which bound us. She wanted me to know about her life so that I might be wiser for all the information. She believed that if wisdom had a colour it would be red and that we would always be bonded by red because it represented happiness.

My mother was an engaging conversationalist. In my pubescent mind, she was both very old and extremely youthful. Her span of historical recall especially in terms of China, was well over a thousand years. Philosophy was her other subject. She always added her social perception, humour and emotional understanding to all ideas and facts. Her best loved dynasties were the Tang and Ming, even though she would refer to the Han for its classical views, always applying them with ease almost as though they were written yesterday. Unfathomably, she was always curious to know my views, and was totally understanding of the reactions from me, however bizarre or naive, incongruous, harmonious, intelligent or ignorant. As I matured gradually during those rebellious years between age fourteen and nineteen, I took her on as my confidante. I felt her wise as Solomon and trusted her with my thoughts and secrets. She was my mother, sister, teacher and my friend. Nobody else engulfed my world nor fascinated me the way she did then. My family and everyone else were only stars in a constellation where she became the North Star. At times I failed to grasp the enormity of the universe from which she had drawn her experience.

Her first encounter with nature was Huangshan or the Yellow Mountain as a child. All she could remember was seeing a sea of clouds as she was taken to one of the peaks to see the clouds from above. It captured her imagination in much the same way as it entered the creative mind of the Chinese since the Tang Dynasty. But it really began with Yuan dynasty monks who built temples on it to become closer to this bewitching landscape. Tang legends foretold of the mountains as a place where immortality or the elixir of youth could be found. Thus through time, painting and poetry has eulogised the mountains, creating a huge body of Chinese art and literature. It went on to develop into the acclaimed 'mountain and water' school of art made famous in the Ming. The natural and cultural impact of these mountains were a part of her. She went there for holidays with her father and always thought that if she did not see them again, something irreplaceable would leave her world forever.

When she was fifteen, my mother was taken on a long sea voyage from Canton to Singapore. As the family sailed out of the harbour, memories of mountain holidays invaded her mind. If there was one thing she would remember of her China, it would be Huangshan. Sketches from the Tang poem ran through her mind:

Morning sun strikes the tree tops
In this sky mountain world,
Chinese people, raise your faces
For a thousand years cranes come and go…
An ocean in the sky
A peak lost in a sea of cloud….
Thousands of feet high towers the yellow Mountains
With its thirty-two magnificent peaks
Blooming like lotus flowers….

Her father repetitiously reminded her not to worry about the mountains and to focus on the new adventures ahead. Details of that arduous migration were unimaginable. Sometimes recalling a book I read about the journey of a Chinese Mandarin, his family and thirty crew in fiction, I could visualise parallels with what happened during my mother's trip from China. Her family were fleeing a country gripped by civil war and foreign invasion. Her father, my grandfather, was Han Chinese, one who was astute and erudite. His name was Loke Wang-Lei, which means 'a king'. He was proud to describe himself as a gentleman of an ancient lineage and of Ming descent, with ancestors who held on to traditions of reading and writing literature. Being a Mandarin, he must have lost all hope knowing that the best of Chinese culture was in peril. Most of this began with the Boxer Rebellion where the Chinese fought each other from within; simultaneously also battling threatening foreigners with imperialistic interests, representing the enemy without.

In their own devices, they were all fighting for power which was based on trade and profit. It was without civility or respect. Blood seemed to be worthlessly shed for money. At the same time, this was a watershed moment for him as a Mandarin because his role was declining in China. These classic scholars were being replaced by a modern civil service. The era of the Mandarins began around the Zhou Dynasty around the beginning of the sixth century. These scholars were selected by merit through an extremely rigorous imperial examination method mainly based on Confucian philosophy. By the time of the Tang Dynasty, the final form of the Mandarin culture was perfected. Even though the most high-ranking positions were filled by relatives of the emperor and nobility, the Mandarins were the founders and core of the Chinese gentry. Education was the foundation stone for this class of scholars. It became the norm for any governing official, whether in central or state government to be supervised by a Mandarin.

But now their era was at an undisputed end. Further, the country had plunged into economic ruin because of a lack of industrial modernisation which brought with it a shortage of development in strategic military resources and trade. Since the time of the opium wars, foreign powers sought to carve China among them taking advantage of the Chinese weakness to fight back. Finally, civil war was the definitive sign that it was time to leave.

It took my grandfather almost two years to plan the escape because it involved selling property and preparing his two wives and twelve children for a peaceful exodus. There was furniture, books and all the luggage that went along with a large family which had to be packed and moved. There were the other indispensable 'family' members the *amahs* who were the nannies, maids and cooks. These came from a traditional school, and were dressed in *samfoo*, black wide trousers and a white top with Chinese collar and frog buttons. They were nicknamed black and white amahs because of the colours of the uniform they wore. They travelled not only with the equipment for cleaning and cooking, but also brought important ingredients such as herbs and spices which included Sichuan pepper, dried chillies, ginger and saffron. The recruitment of a thirty-man crew and a ship's captain, who knew the type of three masted junk for the long sea voyage, meant that my grandfather needed resourcefulness, tact and mastery of at least three dialects of Chinese.

The foremost thought in his mind was how to establish a new world for himself and his family, away from the vestiges of imperial China. It was preferable to surrendering to Chinese communism which took land ownership away from the gentry. Its ideology attracted leaders who sought to purge the country of the traditional elements of Chinese society, mainly filial piety, the importance of family *and* the importance of education. Fundamental principles such as respect for elders and ancestors were deep rooted in my grandfather's psyche since he was old enough to read about Confucius.

Chinese culture dwelt heavily on respect for one's ancestors. Both Confucianism and Taoism held the belief that family is viewed as a closely united group of living and dead relatives. Ancestor worship consists of making offerings to the dead in order to keep them happy in return for blessings from them. More importantly in Chinese culture the function of this was to cultivate kinship values like filial piety, family loyalty, and the continuation of the family lineage.

On leaving China his thoughts were not so much about his ancestors nor the importance of where they were buried, even though *that* had weighed heavily on his mind. He understood his past but now in a boat navigating the perilous sea in South China, his present circumstances forced him to pray for his future. Far from thoughts about the dead his contemplation was focused on the living. The traditional importance of the family and how much he loved his, and thus felt responsible for each member's life, were among the deliberations that went on and on in his mind. On reaching some conclusion, he turned it over again. It was both instinctive and intuitive. As he looked and talked to them often at dinner during the journey, his private thoughts were often focused on how they were sailing into a great unknown. However he knew that at least he had moved them away from certain death.

My mother had inherited his clarity of thought and boldness in decision making. The perilous crossing of the South China Sea helped sharpen his mind for the negotiation with the English bureaucracy in Singapore, the point of entry to the Straits Settlements of Malaya. His knowledge of English and his ability to speak it well had been drummed into him by a kind missionary teacher in Canton. Importantly, she taught him that overall it was respect for a foreign country that gave one the will to learn its language. He understood that as he attempted to read Dickens and Shakespeare. They were experiences that first exploded in him, but with time improved his mind.

Though only fifteen, my mother was his favourite child because she had an imaginative and open spirit. He also appreciated her courage and adventurous soul because he had not seen that in her older brothers and sisters.

He discussed literature with her mainly to help her understand the beliefs, customs and experiences of the Chinese throughout history. This provided her with a richer content of vocabulary and guided her to an understanding of the virtues and failings of the human spirit. Much of Chinese literature addresses human values. With her education, he found that he could speak to her openly of his joys but also add a touch of humour to his fears. They laughed over some of the funny aspects of different cultures. Literature unearthed a tolerance and appreciation of cultures. They understood that their new lives needed skills to negotiate between cultural divides they were soon to encounter.

By the time of their arrival, the Straits Settlements had already become a confluence of race and religion. They encountered Tamils with tales from Madras, other cities, villages, and the

India they had left behind. The ethnic Malays had stories to share about their food and even chillier stories about the ghosts that ran around in the countryside. The Chinese were divided between those who stayed on as merchants in the ports such as Singapore, and the entrepreneurs who went further into the country to develop tin mines or plant rubber in plantations. There were rumours and tales about these adventurers and their exploits. They also regrouped according to the Chinese dialects they spoke, mainly Cantonese and Hokkien, Teochew, Hakka and Hokchew. Many of them had to learn two or three dialects in order to speak to their staff. My mother and grandfather spoke mainly in Mandarin and Cantonese. He trained her to be prepared for all aspects of the journey by road. He used Chinese stories, almost as parables, to teach her new ideas of tolerance and empathy. He taught her to be rooted in the past but to be unafraid of new cultures. In many ways he simply taught her how to think for herself in a clear and positive way.

As they made that second long land journey from Singapore to the northern Straits Settlement of Penang, they learnt Hokkien rapidly, as it was widely spoken by the new recruits in the company. They travelled by road in three cars and a series of heavy lorries, virtually in convoy. He had purchased all the vehicles in Singapore and planned the expedition meticulously. The journey of four hundred miles was divided into three parts, each taking a week. The stops had been advised by Chinese friends who had consulted their English friends. The relationship between the English and the Chinese was tense because there was little trust, and mainly because English law curtailed their entrepreneurial instincts. The British knew the whole country well because they administered it. They also appreciated that each race had a contribution to make to the development of the country. The Chinese who wanted the commerce were the owners of most of the businesses in the small towns. These were on a north-south road trunk road running from Singapore to Penang.

My mother was fascinated by the names of those towns, unpronounceable in the Chinese tongue; Johor Bahru, Muar,

Batu Pahat, Malacca. Then she would come across something more familiar like Yong Peng. There were also names one had to make a point to write down because otherwise it would simply be forgotten; Tanjong Malim, Bidor, Kampar, and Paloh or Ipoh. They were named after rivers which had Malay names. Nothing had been done the Chinese way, which was confusing to her. The Chinese named their cities according to the lay of the land where they were founded. In this way, the topographical map of China produced cities which were related to rivers, mountains, and other natural features, of which her favourite was 'upon the sea'(Shanghai). But her best-loved name was Taiping, which meant eternal peace. In her imagination the name was poetic, romantic and idealistic; nothing to do with topography. It was located in the foothills of the range of mountains that formed the backbone of peninsula Malaya. From the top of the peak of Maxwell they could view ranges of mountains as far as the eye could see. If they could imagine, well it felt as if they had never left China and the Yellow Mountains. My grandfather decided it should be in this town called Taiping, that he would build a new house for his daughter.

First that the town was set beneath the Maxwell Hills, enchanted his daughter. My grandfather went up the foothills in a sedan chair. From there he looked down and saw that the *feng shui* of the town below was almost perfect. Feng Sui literally means wind and water, and in ancient times landscapes and bodies of water were thought to direct the universal Qi, through favourable places. Because Qi has the same patterns as wind and water, then if you live in an area of good Qi, there will be health, wealth and harmonious living.

As fate dictated, they would put down roots in a strange new country, to begin another life. He had dreams and visions, but when they were finally in their house with the lotus ponds beneath the hills; he could believe that his daughter would have a life far better than one he ever imagined for her in their homeland.

CHAPTER TWO

The House With The Lotus Ponds

One of my earliest conversations with my mother was about the voyage from China. I could never predict what she would say next. I adored it that her mind was so open and full of opinion but systematically reserved. It was almost as though she was storing up information and thoughts, for the right time to expose and debate them. I remember vividly the tilt of her head to the right; eyes wide open staring into space as if to recall time; evoking the heat and fragrance that moment must have brought by elegant hand gestures. Sometimes pondering, with her top right-hand finger resting on the corner of her mouth. Her hands were so delicate and slim. She wore rings and filigree gold bracelets. We were eating lotus seeds peeling them from their pods. They were fresh, white and delicious.

'We had the gardeners dig ponds in our garden so that we could grows these, you know,' said my mother quietly in between small mouthfuls.

'Were the lotus plants in the back of the house? Just before the gardens?' I said.

'No beyond the gardens so that the problem with mosquitoes was not so great,' she replied.

Saving the lotus ponds for last, she first described the house her father had built in Taiping. It was constructed mainly of timber. The wood was mahogany and teak. It was designed in the local style of big family mansions in Malaya in the 1930s. Built from an amalgam of dissonant yet harmonious architectural styles, it was an elegant colonial mansion of that period. There were dark wooden beams and walls. The concrete and stone work was painted white. It was her father's idea to have the timber stained a dark brown, almost black. It had a pitched roof with overhanging eaves, decorated in the Chinese style, for the rain. The high roofs allowed for good ventilation that drew in the cool air. There were side balconies and a portico with masonry plinths and timbered columns. The doors were carved in wood with dragons and phoenixes writhing in the Chinese tradition. The ground floor was wide and spacious and it became the reception rooms and playroom for the children when the weather was bad. There were tiled floors both for the coolness and beauty. Some of these tiles had travelled with them from the ancestral home in China.

'My father had a special Chinese room where he hung these huge, beautiful ancestral portraits of his mother and father. There was also his collection of Ming porcelain including incense burners with lemon grass incense to keep the mosquitos at bay,' she continued.

'Did he ever tell you he missed China?' I asked.

'No, he did not. In his stoic way he did not indulge in nostalgia. The past was over; and however glorious, the present and future was where one would look to.' she replied.

'And he surrounded himself with beauty,' I said,

'His collection of Ming court porcelain, furniture, art, his books and a new gramophone player playing the latest jazz from Europe. Ours was probably the only house for miles blasting out the new sound of syncopated rhythms from Paris,' she added excitedly

'A modern Mandarin, with some knowledge of Hindu and Malay culture and but a domineering appreciation for modern French music,' I said, excitedly.

'Not domineering, just enthusiastic. Our home in Taiping was always bursting with new ideas from Europe and England. My father loved the way the infrastructure was planned in the Malayan towns by the English; education first and foremost, followed by transport, communications, finally law and order,' she said.

Knowing how close they were, my mother probably understood the nuances of her father's delight and his disappointment of some of life's situations. Further, she developed his adaptability which was a coping mechanism in a new country. He would go on to buy several houses to overlook his rubber plantations to the north of Taiping, but the house with the lotus ponds would be where he would share his best hours with her and her siblings. His various possessions were meticulously and aesthetically arranged by him in the three living rooms and his bedroom. His wife saw the running of the kitchen and amahs' quarters. These quarters were a row of rooms joint to the main house by a roofed walk. The big garden of magnolia, bamboo and jasmine also had other tropical plants such as hibiscus, and trees which were planted as 'experiments', such as the yellow meranti. Overall, the garden was planted as a traditional Chinese garden with rocks, a small pavilion, trees and flowers.

'The lotus ponds were very much the water element,' said my mother, 'to balance out and produce the harmony of the place.'

'Did your brothers and sisters appreciate the pond?' I asked.

'No the boys were off on their bikes after their tutors had dismissed them, always to the local botanical gardens just a short distance away. And mainly to be with their friends. So we were left on our own to play on the grass and watch the carp in the water. They were idyllic days,' she said with a big, quizzical smile.

'Did you have many friends?' I asked, inquisitively.

'Yes. My mother encouraged that because she wanted us to settle down in our new country. Although our friends were mainly Chinese girls. Occasionally we would ask one or two Malay and Indian friends from school to join us. When they were around, English would be spoken. Otherwise we spoke in Cantonese which was the popular dialect in Taiping.' she said explaining meticulously.

'What did you talk about?' I said excitedly.

She did not directly answer that question but would then explain in detail the various activities and games which whiled away time. She said it was hard to imagine that suddenly it would be evening and the amahs would spoil the moment by insisting that everyone went home. In such a magical garden one of their best loved games was 'Go Find'. They took turns to be the 'head'. This head person could then say 'Go find the smallest leaf,' or 'Go find the most beautiful flower,' etc. and then proceed to judge the offerings. This simple game developed their imagination for the beauty of the place and a love for nature in it.

The varieties of lotus that they would grow in the pond multiplied mainly because of the delight for the flowers that came from my mother. This was whispered to her father whose ear she had. He would then direct the gardener, a young Tamil man from Kerala. Samu was an amateur botanist, but an expert at procreating plants and trees, flowers, shrubs and grass, mosses and vegetables. It was from him that my mother would develop a love for growing orchids when she had a garden of her own. Samu could grow anything from seeds or cuttings. He was probably one of the most important persons in her father's new world because like him, he was also obsessed with plants.

It was in explaining about Samu that she came round to talking about her father's passion for growing lotus. He had brought with him amongst all his treasures, lotus seeds. He knew approximately what the growing conditions were going to be like in the Straits Settlements and was thrilled about its tropical weather. In his scholarly and fertile mind, he imagined ponds of white, yellow, pink and blue flowers. Revered in China as a sacred flower, the water lily above all symbolised the purity of the mind and heart. Through stories and fables, it characterised honour, health, longevity and good fortune.

She briefly spoke about Homer and the lotus eaters in the *Odyssey*, of how Homer told that Odysseus could not get his ship's crew back onto the boat for its return to Ithaca. And of how warrior soldiers were hooked on lotus seeds. She explained how mythology did not dwell too much on real facts. Contradicting Homer, my mother explained that the only way a person could become hallucinated from lotus was perhaps to smoke the petals of the blue lotus, which had to be first dried.

She explained that far away from the Greek islands, the Chinese would have been eating lotus for over a thousand years. The succulent seeds were eaten fresh or boiled, the roots made a delicate soup and the petals were used to flavour stews. Most of all, the lotus was not eaten but appreciated for its beauty.

The white flower was often associated with purity, whilst the yellow stood for enlightenment and therefore revered by Buddhists. The blue lotus was known for its petals which had mild aphrodisiac and psychedelic properties. It was known as the dream flower. Chinese poets have written endlessly about its creative power and purity; its tenacity to grow in adverse surroundings. In literature it was symbolic of the seventh month, summer; thus inspiring countless Chinese minds to weather storms and difficulties simply by being aware of life's seasons by observing nature. It led to this innate tenacity to show their best selves to the outside world.

The house with the lotus ponds made an indelible impression on my mother, not only because of the man with the sound of jazz but also for his flowers of enchantment that grew in abundance for them.

CHAPTER THREE

Foreigners

My mother's attitude towards foreigners was one of respect. Her father had spent time studying the Chinese psyche through literature and discourse. He had come to a vague conclusion that there would always be some mistrust of the 'ghost' people because of the pale color of their skin. But he was obsessed about the new skills they brought in both commerce and military strategy, and thus counselled his daughter to keep her views about race open. He was adamant that both he and his children should learn about the 'foreign' people. They were nicknamed the '*qwei-lo*' or foreign devils. There was a wide belief from his father before him that China was the 'Middle Kingdom' or '*Zhongguo*'. The Chinese believed that their favourable location, placed in the middle of the world, was advantageous for the control of power. Since the kingdom of the Chou, 3000 years ago, they believed that theirs was the only civilised empire and that they were surrounded by barbarians. Not until the eighteenth century did some of China's Mandarins wake up to the fact that they were only innovators of some important products, but no longer in admired for their position in the world.

'The Chinese are instinctively xenophobic,' my mother suddenly said one day in the middle of having tea with me.

I was fifteen. We were sitting on the verandah of an English tennis club, looking out onto one of the most beautiful gardens I can remember. It was a good time for this sensitive conversation because with such a halcyon view, it seemed possible that everything negative could be turned into something positive with friendly debate.

'Which is why there was a mistrust of foreigners even when they came with good intentions and were civilised,' I replied.

'Yes. And the racial prejudice for these foreign imperialists was real because they feared being subjugated to another culture, especially a Westernised one,' she replied awkwardly.

This was genuinely a difficult topic for her to discuss. Being in the Taiping Club, we were definitely enjoying one of the benefits the British had created in Malaya. But there was always some reason for mistrust of the qwei-lo. She told me that an

Englishman kept running up huge debts in one of the shops owned by her brother, assuming that credit was due to him as a matter of form.

She then gave me a short discourse on how the Chinese had pursued the idea of keeping the Chinese race pure in order to ensure the longevity of its culture. Wars and killing purged China of foreigners. Confucianism dominated Chinese education from the Han dynasty to the Tang, the Ming and the Qing. Central to this was the language. There were up to a hundred dialects in China. The predominant dialect, standard Chinese, is based on Mandarin Chinese; often referred to as the first language because more than seventy percent of the population understood it. Cantonese came second and it was spoken in the populous Guangzhou province and its surrounding area.

'So, what in a few words, does Chinese culture mean to you, Confucius aside?' I asked delicately.

'Oh many things; pride in the longevity of Chinese civilisation, in our ingenuity to invent things such as paper, silk, printing, the compass, etc., and pride in our culture of respect for ancestors and family,' she said quickly, almost racing to keep talking.

'So it went beyond drinking tea?' I said in jest.

'Way more than that,' she paused and laughed. 'When we discovered tea, we made the china porcelain teacups and created the whole etiquette of tea pouring,' she said, 'and also the culture of calmness and serenity which comes with offering tea.'

'Yes, in England, the one who pours becomes "mother", a practical gesture, whereas in China you pour tea to show appreciation and respect for the one you serve. With grace and poise, a son or daughter or wife would pour tea for their parents and husbands mainly out of filial piety and respect,' I answered, knowingly.

'But my father was also very pragmatic about the idea of having to integrate into another society and to learn their different ways.' she added eruditely.

'So he studied the social behaviour of the English and tried to understand them?' I answered.

'Yes he had studied the situation of nineteenth century China and how Chinese pride only brought shame,' she said ruefully and spontaneously.

We had discussed the Chinese distrust of foreigners since the Qing dynasty. Yet a few hundred years before that the Ming with positive and forward thinking, had built fleets of ships that would sail to Africa, even around the world. Under Emperor Yongle, the Chinese sent out fleets of roughly sixty vessels per expedition with over 30,000 men. Commanded by Admiral Zhonghe, who oversaw seven expeditions, these 'treasure fleets' would bring back to China ostriches, giraffes and elephants from Africa. They were also laden with rubies, emeralds and diamonds from India and spices including saffron, cinnamon and pepper from the Malay peninsula. But these explorations were suddenly halted.

'The Ming were wrong about their respect for the Confucian world order which held a great disdain for all things connected with trade and money,' she said.

'Ah, an idealised world order does not often work for all things,' I said agreeing with her.

'Yes, he said that the truth lay in the classic virtues of family and good relationships; and a life of education that would finally lead to that truth.' she added.

'Which makes me proud of my heritage,' I said.

'But you cannot live in that sort of ivory tower forever because the world comes knocking on your door,' she continued.

She knew that the Chinese had reached a stage when they became too confident in their civilisation. They failed to develop on their own innovations. These were many, but among the most important, gunpowder and paper were used as tools for the military and economic expansion by the Western powers. Chinese Qing politics was also outmoded. The wealthy Mandarins, the scholarly bureaucratic class allowed themselves to be affected by the whims and wiles of the emperor and the glory of the imperial court. Clearly, traditional Confucian thinking proved too narrow and such an inward thinking mindset put them in jeopardy with the outside world. The Opium Wars were preceded by a time when the English East India company was at its zenith. Unwittingly the Chinese traded inexpensive opium from British India for silk, tea and silver. Opium was an Achilles heel and China paid a heavy price for that vulnerability in money and war. There were uprisings from the farmers who were forced to pay higher taxes and a rising spectre of urban revolts. These occurred when the people in towns were anxious that famine would occur because of falling food supplies from a distressed agricultural sector

'My father remembers those times as the most tumultuous. The people were disturbed and wrathful. We frequently forget how big the population of China was, even then,' she said with a sigh.

'I cannot imagine living in a world where there was a shortage of food, it's so naive, I know,' I answered.

'That's why we made that long journey. To settle in a place where there was enough fertile land and where there will always be an abundance of everything, especially food.'

'But do you hate the English?' I added quickly.

'On the contrary, I rather admire the English. Look at the British Empire. It was built on progressive thinking, cunning and courage. It had to be so well organised and cleverly governed. They spread the spirit of law and order and further, imposed that. Sent their governors, bureaucrats, professional civil servants, entrepreneurs, sometimes their brightest and best men, out of England to live in strange places.' she said. 'They had the boldness to take chances in order to increase the resources of their small island race. My father greatly appreciated that kind of audacity.

'The Pearl River Delta was a malarial swamp in China,' I said intelligently.

'So was Butterworth in Malaya and all those towns in India; there was stink and rubbish which brought diarrhoea, cholera, along with the mosquito diseases. The average life expectancy was twenty-five!' she said, expecting to continue on talking about this.

'In a way they thought in reverse of how the Chinese people were thinking. They proudly spread the English language and culture in trade, in a way that the Chinese failed to do with theirs, mainly because they felt that others were too inferior to appreciate it,' she said.

And here I recognised the argument that I would cherish for the rest of my life. That a civilisation like China would grow despite its reversal of fortunes from time to time. It has a long history with the past to which it clings tenaciously and automatically because the Chinese psyche remains stubborn to its culture. George Orwell put it elegantly *'Who controls the past controls the future. But who controls the present controls the past.'* It was so different to the English attitude to civilisation

'But we applaud that too. They fought for God, glory and gold. Which I understand. In the Chinese scheme of things their ancestors were their idea of glory. That was worth fighting for and grounding themselves in what they believed to be their truth,' she said. 'We got round that by coming to a totally foreign country and adopting some of that English way of life and making it work to the Chinese advantage,' she finally said.

Her father was a visionary who bred that same imagination in his daughter. She relied on her intuition and creativity, especially in dealing with people of different cultures. Her inventiveness was a constant source of inspiration to all who knew her. She lived her life with a great sense of adventure and fearlessness because in her core, she was true to herself. I admired her purity, her strength and her perception. Far from being a classic refugee; I imagined that she sank her roots in deep; and was like some fabled rain tree which sprouted into the sky and blossomed bright yellow flowers which produced seed in pods that glowed like Chinese lanterns.

CHAPTER FOUR

Gold Plates

As with all selective memory, my mother remembered only the best years of her life. She received a good education from one of the mission schools in Taiping where the curriculum was taught in English. Her father bought two rubber plantations of a few thousand acres, one to the north towards Penang, the other to the south towards Ipoh. He had houses built in these towns for his sons who were trained to take over the business. He first hired experienced Chinese managers whom he trusted to look after the rubber estates. From the very beginning he hired professional European planters to supervise the planting and early operations of the plantations.

'Did your father talk about his problems on becoming a planter?' I asked.

'Overall he had thought about it for many years and developed many friends. He had the mind of an entrepreneur but above all he was always curious. He experimented with different types of businesses. In the beginning he bought many shops, one selling sports equipment, one was a photographic studio and he even bought a small cinema showing films he rented,' she said.

'Ah, he was into the leisure business,' I laughed.

'Yes, but many of these failed. It was after a few years of being in Malaya that he forged the plan to plant rubber and to be in the plantation business,' she added.

She also talked in depth about her father's wealth because he confided in her. She was, by now almost twenty and good at mathematics. They calculated all costs and profits on an abacus, doing all their own accounting and bookkeeping. Budgeting for a growing family and family business was all carefully worked out on separate ledgers for cash, customer deposits, investments and cash payments. Her father had learnt all these in all very rudimentary way before he left China. There was little time to learn because the subject of business management was yet unknown but he had a natural flair as a businessman. Now more than ever in strange new surroundings he knew he only had himself and his instincts to trust.

He had envisioned rubber planting mainly because he had five sons. Land was very cheap. The British residents and Malay sultans almost gave acres of jungle away to encourage development. The cost of foreign labour for Tamil tappers was low. He had been advised to build accommodation for his workers together with all the production facilities for processing latex. The housing infrastructure was known as 'lines'. As the word described, the houses were built and laid out in lines with streets in between. Often included with the housing, were communal kitchens and bathrooms, a primary school and nursery for children, together with medical facilities and shops, thus creating all the facilities needed for a population of over one thousand people. Resident estate managers were either Chinese or English. Their bungalows were usually built on higher ground often overlooking the estate. Estates were run almost as small towns adapting British law and order to local entrepreneurial skills.

'Rubber required so much investment and organisational skills because they grew the plants from seedling and that took seven to eight years before they could even begin to tap the trees,' my mother said.

'And I would guess before one could plant anything it took ages to clear the virgin jungle first,' I said.

'Yes, then mapping out an estate with roads, housing, and a factory where the rubber latex could be turned into sheet rubber. It had to be professionally planned. It took sheer dedication and hard graft. But planting was in my father's blood, whether he was creating a garden or a plantation,' she added.

'I admire that strength of character, did he also show you the plantation, in all it's different stages?' I asked.

'It was not really a place for a young woman. Apart from the risk of being raped, the jungle was quite dangerous. I remember when I went for a walk in it on a narrow path. We were a party of six men and myself,' she said beginning one of her long stories.

'And what happened?' I added.

'I was trying to be brave but I was terrified of tigers and snakes. I nearly stepped on a blackish patch when the estate manager stopped my foot from hitting the ground. It was a gigantic scorpion measuring over a foot long with his tail up ready to sting. They put it in a box and took it home. It turned out that he collected scorpions. And butterflies,' she concluded.

There were many more recollections of how she studied the animal life in dense vegetation. She came to terms with its savagery and turned to observe the tropical forest for its unique immense diversity in flora and fauna. She kept notebooks of the leaves and flowers she pressed. Her best tales however was about plantation life. It meant waking up really early but never early enough to see the tappers come in with their big cans of latex rubber. They would have gone out well before five in the morning, wearing little candles or lamps on their caps. Most of the tapping was completed before the fiery tropical sun rose. She constantly stared at their sweaty faces and marvelled at their craft of cutting the bark of the rubber tree delicately on a slant deep, enough to release the milky fluid that oozed into a tiny cup at the base of the cut.

Tapping was such a skilled job because the tree would survive for over twenty-eight years if this was done well. The tappers were strong and hardy because their job was done in darkness, with their little lights focused on their hands and the sharp blades they held. She would at times walk out with her father into the plantation in the morning. She shared his sense of wonder at these huge cathedrals of trees and the lingering smell of the liquid they produced. It gave him purpose and a great sense of belonging which she soon adopted.

The sense of belonging seemed like such a fundamental human need, much like a need for shelter or for food. It had an important bearing in seeing the value of life and coping with painful emotions. Strange though it was, belonging became an instinctive way in which they organised themselves in their new country. It became a paramount objective and focus. My mother discussed this at great lengths but spoke about it almost as her allegory of how her father made the long spiritual journey out of China. He migrated with the future of his family in his mind. Subconsciously he found himself constantly deleting nostalgic memories of China. He instinctively knew that in other to see open doors, he had to close others. He recalled part of the poem by Wang Bo

....And yet, when China holds our friendship
And heaven remains our neighbourhood
Why should you linger at the fork of the road
Wiping your eyes like a broken-hearted child?....

But he hungered for the smell of pine trees and raw earth. He only had to think of the Huangshan mountains in the mist, those yellow granite grotesque peaks with green pine trees jutting out at odd angles, and it would bring a smile, sometimes the odd tear. Or the trips he took with his father down the Yangtze River on river boats. Elegant cities like Suzhou with its meandering canals, bridges and classical landscaped gardens. He knew he had left a part of himself in all these places. But in his mind and his books; when he had time to read poetry, these places were conjured up magically. He felt that he could travel to the far ends of the earth but still retain the memory of them vividly.

'It was when we started the plantation project that my father really believed that he had left China. In his mind and spirit he had begun the process to settling down in the foreign but beautiful Malaya. He had come to terms with forgetting the past and was proud that he was able to provide for and to protect his family,' she said poignantly.

'It was such forward and courageous thinking,' l replied.

'In all those ten to fourteen years, I do not think he had much time to reflect. He was riding into the wind. He knew how to keep his head down and to simply embrace the wind. I was very lucky…' she paused.

'To have been the daughter he loved and to whom he told everything,' I said quickly.

'He had such confidence, yes, even the audacity, to believe that what he was doing was good and productive. For such long-term decisions, his simple plan was always to be happy with the day,' she reflected.

She always developed her own contemplation, adding on and taking away, as if to construct in her mind something of a model father and man. There were other conversations on subjects which ranged from the most mundane, like what he had eaten for dinner, to other more serious matters which verged on life, death and economic chaos. Because of his background in Chinese literature, he would also teach her and discuss the classics, fully aware that her future education would not include Chinese poetry from the Tang dynasty. He also taught her to write Mandarin Chinese using Chinese characters. Despite the large differences among Chinese dialects, these all shared the same writing system based on Chinese characters. There were over 70,000 characters from which a scholar could draw. These rather special occasions were imprinted in my mother's young mind. From this would germinate her own ideas on how civilised she thought her father's culture was, and the privilege it gave her for being able to share it.

One day he showed her twelve golden plates, and two others which were adorned with blue enamel. He explained that they were from the Ming period and a farewell present from an aunt before leaving China. She was absolutely breathless when she held them. Each one represented one of his twelve children and the two emblazoned in cloisonné stood for himself and his wife. The cloisonné *Jingtai blue ware*' was enamel work and very special to the Chinese. They had improved on enamel ware made in the Byzantine Empire, which had travelled to China via the Silk Road. He also told my mother that he believed that the base metal of the blue plates was gold. Those gold plates were sentimental to him.

'It was not exactly Proust from *A la Recherche de temps perdu*, you know, in 'remembrance of things past,' I said.

'No, the French can be so absurdly tragic,' she replied. 'The Chinese admire the passing of time because of the inspiration it brings to the future,' she added.

'We have this wonderful tradition of celebrating the best times of our life in the hope that the future might produce even better experiences ,' I said.

'And lay the ghost of bad experiences,' she replied.

So we continued on one of the many mother-to-daughter exchanges on differences in the state of the world. She pressed on to deliberate about how French view the loss of time and often equated this as a loss to the present meaning of life. This was so different to Chinese perception of time. All time was precious because generally, the Chinese think in the long term. This encouraged the ability to persevere and invest in time.

The meaning of the gold plates to her father was enlightened by his way of thinking. In time, they would come to represent the wealth in his own personal growth. There was no issue of losing. In this foreign land he was aware of the new positive relationships he had to forge and how these depended on his intelligence, goodwill, tolerance and kindness. He was seeking that final goal; not only in the big and obvious, but in his own tranquil ability to enjoy small and ordinary things that brought him joy.

But to his daughter there was always a long-term view represented by a stubborn and passionate man. She recognised his tendency to control the environment which suggested a remarkable grit that was the product of a need to adapt to changing circumstances. The fact that he was able to see the Maxwell peaks and make believe they resembled his beloved Yellow Mountains was a remarkable way of carrying on with his life in order to achieve the larger goals he had set for himself. He often spoke of the Confucian proverb that 'a crisis was just an opportunity of riding a dangerous wind.'

CHAPTER FIVE

A Western Education

My mother inherited the sense of stubborn perseverance from her father. The dangerous journey from China had also given her an acute sense of survival. Physically it was an arduous time but that taught her valuable lessons keeping her body fit and healthy. As she was growing into a beautiful young woman, men looked at her in a different way, and strangely it was her father who taught her how to conduct herself modestly and purely. Their closeness, through the tough voyage and into a new alien country gradually expanded her mind exponentially in different directions. She was not as keen to find a husband and have babies. From an early age she had mapped out her own vision statement. She would often look up into a night sky and wonder of its infinity, and think that there must be something she could create to improve the lives of others.

'My mind started to create its own sense of meaning to life,' said my mother one day when we started to talk of her career and goals.

'Yes, the young see visions, you must have been really close to your father to have such maturity,' I said.

'He loved me and simply wanted me to be someone extraordinary,' she said

'It is strange how he did not become close to one of his sons,' I interjected.

'Yes, they were all genetically hardwired to be like him but they did not have his sensitivity or earnest desire to bring about or to accept change,' she said.

'How could they not see change? Everything was changing around them,' I said not, really understanding.

'That was the problem. They were all fazed and traumatised by how much their world had changed,' she said.

'You were about the only one of his children who were excited of being in a new country,' I replied.

'Yes, I was thrilled at the idea of new places, ideas and the challenges they brought,' she said.

Then she started to tell me about how a privileged childhood had influenced her in a positive way. She felt that in some way she could use her mind and body to change the world. She decided either to be a doctor or a teacher. During those days between the two world wars she was encouraged to be at home with her parents and help out responsibly with her sisters. She trained under the '**normal**' teacher training courses established by the English government in Malaya to become a primary school teacher. Those days before her marriage, were halcyon days. She was young, beautiful, and rich with her father's help. Apart from things intellectual, she had her youthful foibles and especially an indulgence in clothes.

'I can't believe you were a fashion plate,' I said suddenly interested in the conversation.

'Yes I was very stylish and looked to how modern Hong Kong women were transforming the old classic *cheongsam* into something wearable and suitable to the working woman,' she continued.

'Do you mean you wore the cheongsam to work? Chinese women were probably only wearing Western clothes,' I interjected.

'Yes. Everyday. I never really thought there was problem between the East and the West, whether or not it was the clothes I wore, or the attitude I had. I was always myself.' she continued.

'Progressive and looking forward,' I said.

'Always be yourself *nui, nui,*' she said. She used the Chinese word for daughter as a term of endearment.

Apart from that short moment, she hardly ever indulged in trivial matters. Instead we often had long serious discussions on what her father had said about Chinese education. He emphasised how the Eastern way of education was centred on more than a thousand years of literature. Literature was the means to teach people how to live virtuously. In the abstract, it also encouraged a life lived more harmoniously with nature. He noticed that Western education was more progressive. While they retained their classics, they used education for national reform. Western philosophy transformed education. Seats of learning produced the Enlightenment and the Industrial Revolution.

These meant that in relative terms compared to the West, Chinese society had stagnated. China was stuck in the

'Mean', the Confucian way of looking at a harmonious ...n striving to memorise classical works and to share the .... on they produced. In the West the centre of gravity had moved from learning to analysis and innovation; and finding a rate of return on the investment. This advanced state produced thinkers such as Jean-Jacques Rousseau and John Locke. In general, theirs was a belief that the world depended on quantitative thinking, which was generally the ability to think clearly and rationally about what to do and what to believe. This gave way to the ability to understand how to make the logical connection between ideas. It gave rise to a burst of thousands of new ideas which kept expanding exponentially.

Many Chinese like my grandfather left China because they were disillusioned at the 'qualitative' thinking which kept the Chinese stuck at a point of history which still adhered to Confucian philosophy. On this platform of strict ancient rules, they were forbidden to look to a creative expansion in other forms of ideology especially those focusing on social and political reform. Most critical thinking and problem solving was restricted to the confines of Taoist and certain Confucian thinking. My mother's world opened because her father *had* decided that western thought and the freedom of an individual to make up his own mind was key to individual progress and sociopolitical enhancement. There had been an illegal infiltration of some important foreign books, but he knew that the time had come for him to leave China when these were actually burnt by officials. Book burning had existed in China for millennia since the first emperor Qin Shi Huangdi had burnt Confucian texts which opposed the ideas he held on ruling China.

'I never quite understood why they burnt books in China,' I said to my mother.

'It was a demonstrative way of stopping all radical thinking. Since Shi Huangdi, books were burnt to stop these books from having any impact on the next generation's thoughts,' she replied clearly.

'So there is always this idea of censorship in order to control how you thought?' I added.

'This idea of forbidding free thought to be heard or to acquire new knowledge burned in my father's mind for years; until it became unbearable to live under such control,' she ended.

She had evolved in her mind the idea of a building a school as a dedication to her father's life. Though his life was devoted to Chinese learning, he was fascinated with the radical progress made in Western thought with regards education. Western education was focussed on the student's motivation to search for new information, generate questions and formulate ideas.

Even mistakes made it possible to get a better understanding of the problem. Thus intellectuals and philosophers in the West were fighting old unjust privileges, intolerance and even misgovernment. Schools and universities were expected to promote literacy and mental discipline to prepare students not only for citizenship but individual development. In China the emphasis on learning Confucian classics and memorising them by rote dismissed individual thought. The vital role of an Eastern education was to bring honour to the families and society. It instilled in children a deep sense of the collective good.

My mother knew that her father had written about East/West differences and raised concerns that a Confucian education would serve little purpose if one had to adapt to a modern world. Most important of all he had long discussions with his daughter about the relevance of individual thought. She must have decided to run with all his ideas. The school she had envisaged would have a Western curriculum and thus be able to give students a Western education. In her studies in training to become a primary school teacher, she was amazed that children were taught to not only have reading and writing skills but also to develop physical, social, emotional, cultural and cognitive skills. The last drew her attention mainly because it meant that children were taught to reason logically. This idea would have been dismissed in China.

CHAPTER SIX

Becoming Susan

For a long while my mother was uncomfortable with her name. She was convinced it sounded like a boy's name and was adamant that her father had chosen it because he had wished for a boy. She was called 'glorious defender', which was what her name Loke Sau-San meant. She had asked her mother about the choice but was given the answer that it was always up to the men to decide, which infuriated her even more. Her father had explained how he had a curious admiration for Chinese women who were trained to fight. She also knew from him how patriarchal Chinese society was. It was also patrilineal, in the sense that descent was through the male line. Since the eleventh century, this prejudiced preference led to high rates of female infanticide. Practices such as foot binding was a strong tradition up to the Qing Dynasty and was focused on the masculine dominance over woman's rights. It represented the control to restrict the freedom of movement of women, especially those in upper class echelons.

Throughout the long odyssey voyage from China, father and daughter bonded. This relationship became strong enough for him to reveal to her some of his innermost feelings. These included speaking about his love for his family especially his wife and daughters. He also showed his contempt for those men who mistreated women because they were physically weaker or less able to protect themselves because they were not provided with the skills to earn money. He believed that women should be financially independent in the world. He reassured her that he would teach her all that he knew first, to protect the money that she would inherit from him, but also to find her own voice in the world. In this way he had wished her life to be extraordinary.

Often he recounted stories of the heroines of Chinese history, in awe of the lives they had lived, because they had acquired abilities and led remarkable lives. He remembered the Tang emperor who paid his daughter the greatest tribute by including music at her funeral. When officials objected, he complimented his daughter by simply replying, 'She was not an ordinary woman.'

'Did you ever ask him why he gave you such a masculine name?' I asked her when we came to our renowned 'yin-yang' conversation.

'No, no, I never raised that question,' she answered.

'So was he genuine in his respect for women?' I asked curiously.

'Yes, my father adored women and admired them. Not only did he love their feminine ways; for their kind heartedness, gentleness, loyalty and humane wisdom. He loved their nuances, how they would support men and their seeming lack of ego in doing so. But above all he loved them for their courage,' she said.

'Did he appreciate strong women?' I asked willing her to continue.

'Yes and by that he really meant the ones who were educated but also had the ability and the confidence to defy the norm,' she said.

'Thus not in the usual Confucian, yin-yang tradition,' I said glibly.

We would carry on discussing how even though there was social inequality between gender, this was not reflected strongly in the culture's philosophical thought. Most Chinese thinkers paid homage to the advantageousness of the complimentary nature of male and female characteristics. In the Mengzi texts in the fourth century BC, it was written that 'the greatest human relationship is that a man and a woman could live together.' It explained the difference between male and female qualities, but believed that each has its particular positive aspects to offer. Basically these traits are complementary and therefore can be unified to form a harmonious whole. She would continue to reflect that though her father did not talk much about his relationship with his wife, he exuded the confidence of a happy husband.

'I was not really interested in what he would say about my mother,' she said suddenly.

'Yes, I can understand that. After all that is a private matter. Did he talk intimately about Chinese women at all?' I asked.

'No, there remained the bits that were mysterious to him but overall they fascinated him. He always went back to history. I remember how he was enthralled by the high status of urban women who were assertive and active in the presence of men during the Tang Dynasty. The courtesans who wore gold headdresses and ornate combs and pearls, and were made up with powder. They were singers and poets. They threw banquets and feasts, knew all the rules of social drinking and had the most respectable table manners,' she replied clearly.

'And the energetic Tang women also played polo in trousers,' she added.

'Yes with defiance to rules and danger. Like me when I think of Alexander the Great, I am intrigued by this handsome warrior who was able to command an army of 50,000 men to go into battle to defeat the Persians, a force three times the size of his own. He also found time to spread Greek culture in faraway places, such as Anatolia and the Ionic coast. He built temples to the Greek gods all along his journey which ended in India,' I continued.

'There were many Chinese women warriors who were as great as Alexander,' she began enthusiastically, breaking my attention and subject.

She started by talking of Xun Guang from the western Jin Dynasty in China, around the time Alexander was making his mark in Western Europe. She was a child warrior who went into battle at the age of thirteen and saved her father's city. Legend has it that the city's officials staged a coup against him, the governor, by laying siege. With a group of soldiers she broke through enemy lines to reassemble reinforcements. She is still widely celebrated in Peking operas.

'So these female warriors had strength and charisma,' I said, thinking of these fragile women going into battle with thousands of men and fighting to defend men.

'Yes I love the psychological aspects of it, to think how strong their minds were to the rebellious beliefs they held. Sometimes there were aspects of honour, but mostly it was the audacity to hope to win *and* having a mindset that women were not weak,' she replied quickly.

My mother continued on about her heroines, beginning with the Empress Wu Zetian of the Tang Dynasty. A concubine of the emperor she fell in love with his son. When he acceded to the throne she confidently declared herself the Empress. She changed the name of the Dynasty to Zhou, thereby giving the Dynasty an automatic extension of China's borders further west.

Her sword-wielding heroine was the warrior Lin Siniang of the Ming Dynasty, who started training when she was four under her father, a master of martial arts. His confidence paid off for him because she led a fully trained all-female army to go in battle to rescue the king. This golden dynasty also produced Qin Liangyu, the only female general to be listed in Chinese dynastic accounts. She was married to a military commander but was renowned for leading the famously known 'White Cavalry' to rescue the Ming emperor in Peking . He was so impressed that he showered her with praises written as poems, as she rode victoriously into the city.

What she loved best was talking about the educated woman she admired most. She was Wang Zhenyi who had fought against the patriarchal customs of eighteenth-century China and won. She educated herself in the fields of mathematics, astronomy, medicine, geography and poetry. Without bitterness for those who criticised her, she wrote poems describing the China she loved.

'She died at twenty-nine,' said my mother.

'To have achieved so much, in such a short time,' I replied quickly.

'She wrote articles on lunar eclipses, the equinoxes and about longitude,' said my mother.

'Did she impress you?' I asked.

'In the beginning, and then she became an inspiration to me,' she added.

'After all, you had one of the best teachers of all,' I said.

'Yes, my father was my teacher and the classroom was the boat on that expedition out of China,' she said slowly but assuredly.

After the first two years in Taiping, my mother decided to change her name. She thought about all the English names she knew from books. There was a Lady Susan in one of Jane Austen's books but that was not the reason my mother chose it. Her maiden name was Sau San and at the drop of one letter she would become Susan. Its origins would be Greek, Persian, Egyptian and Hebrew. And it's meaning would be rose, lily or lotus depending on the country to which one was referring.

In all cases, she was excited by the choice because it would at least describe her femininity. She felt incredibly proud to be a woman. Encouraged by her father of her history and lineage, she had ambitions to become well educated and achieve great things. She was always aware of the family motto, *'Don't be afraid of making changes, be afraid of standing still.'*

CHAPTER SEVEN

Challenges

My mother described her challenges or *tiaozhan*, as filial piety, education, and matrimonial hurdles. She was lucky to be born into wealth and to have had that unusually close relationship with her father. It was more usual for sons to be in the position of running the household. There was staff that took care of running the place and catered to all the meals. Her parents had two maids and a manservant who looked after their every requirement. Mama's natural affiliation with her father grew and she empathised with his need for company and conversations on his favourite subjects. As he became much older, she had no problems deciphering his moods or unravelling his confusions because she knew him so well. She did not achieve this intimacy with her mother, so she left the role of her caring to her sisters. Although he had pretty well put China in the back of his mind, vestiges of his Chinese childhood returned from time to time. My mother saw it as her duty to comfort him with the same anecdotes he had once fascinated her with; hilarious yarns and gripping narratives from the Ming and Tang dynasties. He appreciated her story telling even though he had been the original storyteller. She had grasped their essence and redistilled these chronicles as though she owned them.

She had a woman's interpretation and sometimes he would laugh until he cried, or smiled when he saw the lighter side of the tale. He waited patiently for her daily return, either from a class or a long day in one of his plantations, helping out with the accounts. Knowing whether she had gone by bicycle or driven there in one of his cars including the Ford Model T, he would bide his time either in the front entrance or in one of the side balconies of the house. She also anticipated meeting him after her long day, remembering this lovely man in his silk mandarin tunic and trousers, seated patiently, reading from a small book. They would rush to greet each other with a bow and a wide smile. Hastily a pot of tea, cups and some dainty coconut cakes would appear brought out by one of his servants and served. Very often though, she would compose herself and then reach to pour the tea, as custom dictated, from a younger to an older person out of respect.

After she had finished her secondary school education, my mother could have gone to university in Singapore. Instead, she opted to do a teacher training course named 'normal' run by the English colonial government. These were adapted to a British curriculum. My mother learnt years later that this form of education originated from the French sixteenth century when the concept of '*ecole normale*' was to provide model schools with model classrooms, to teach model teaching practices to its student teachers. Her 'normal' classes were run in Taiping, which meant that she would not be separated from her parents, especially her beloved father. She also took English lessons where she learnt grammar, vocabulary and pronunciation. These lessons were given by a warm-hearted English lady, Mrs. Radcliffe, who did not have a cook. My mother would bring her lunch in a tiffin carrier. This ritual of food gifts began with homemade cakes. At home the family meals consisted of sharing plates of meat, fish and vegetables with rice. The meals at home were elaborate because the family was large. So it was easy allocating some of this food dished into containers. Cantonese cuisine was not renown for desserts but in Malaya with its abundance of coconuts changed that. There were puddings and cakes made of coconut milk, palm sugar and spices from Malay and Indian recipes, which were adapted and elaborated for the Chinese palate.

I often imagined my mother in her youth. As she was so accomplished and beautiful, she must have drawn a crowd of admirers. Ingrained in her was the sense of propriety and correct behaviour. Her parents would have been against an interracial marriage, knowing that the costs were stacked too highly against her. It was difficult to imagine marriage even to a Chinese man because society was still in a state of flux with an inflow of migrants from different countries. There were Cantonese, Hokkien, and other Chinese who had immigrated from the Fujian and Guangzhou provinces.

Although they were mostly Han Chinese, they spoke different dialects of Chinese. But the young professionals who were university educated, spoke mainly English, which was the *lingua franca*, and the language of British Malaya. Her father was anxious that he would be able to communicate to his son-in-law, and insistent that they would be able to speak in English *and* Chinese. My mother agreed vehemently because she respected and loved her father very much. When she was doing her teaching courses there were retreats to the hill town of Cameron Highlands, where she mixed freely with English men and women.

'Were you intrigued by the English?' I asked inquisitively.

'Yes mainly because there was supposedly a cultural chasm between us and they were forbidden fruit,' she said smilingly.

'It must have been strange trying to make friends with the English,' I said.

'It was not at all difficult. The one thing required was a command of the language. Which I had, thanks to Lisa Radcliffe, my beloved English teacher. I made friends easily first with the women and then with men. I think they viewed me as some gifted exotic flower because I spoke to them in their native tongue. My father gave me all the confidence I needed with his attitude of openness and fairness. We hired English planters in one plantation.' she finished.

'And you went to dances and dinners where there was a mixed crowd. Was that exciting?' I asked.

'I just loved the English crowd. They were always less stuffy than the Chinese men. They had a great sense of humour. But I kept my promise to my father, and stayed away from private dates, and kept to large groups!' she laughed.

'Did they hold you close when they danced, you know as in ballroom dancing?' I asked.

'Yes and it was very special, dancing with a handsome Englishman. I was barely eighteen and out in a world where I wanted to know everything and more than that, experience it for myself. But the social structures were rigid. Which I think was good because it kept me out of trouble. For a few years anyway…' she ambled, already thinking of her next story.

'You were totally undaunted, unfazed, by how complicated the world was,' I replied, calmly.

'When you are young you are courageous, no… audacious, because when you see challenges you know no fear as to how you would bring solutions or attack,' she said.

'And like those heroines who rode into battle knowing that they had to do what they were trained for,' I said simply.

'My father had prepared me for life by simply telling me stories of brave deeds and heroism with such conviction,' she continued, pointing to her forehead. 'He didn't leave much room for me to wonder at what I might do. He had prepared my mind for every eventuality it might meet.'

'Like training a warrior,' I answered.

She finally chose a man whom she believed would be a compatible and strong companion in the world. He spoke both Chinese and English and was named Yu Ming Hua. She was initially impressed with the suits he wore. For the daytime he wore off-white linen suits which were made from imported fabric from England. When he dated her in the evenings, he wore white shantung silk jackets with darker linen trousers. He looked the part and been educated in the University of Singapore.

However, he came from a poor family, which was more complex in that his father had several wives and his mother was one of the discarded concubines. Nonetheless mama imagined that he was her fabled hero. And life would turn out as in some of these magical stories. Not a *The Dream of the Red Chamber* tragedy, for her heart was selective. My father knew the moment he met his fiancé that he was not totally eligible. He had a complex about himself and beneath that lay a hidden conflict, even an unexposed demon or two. He kept these secrets to himself, hoping that with marriage, he would learn confidence enough to give his wife the hero she saw in him.

Not quite a year after they were married, the Japanese invaded China. He held his own views about Japan. There had been a cultural bond once between the two nations. The Japanese had adopted much of Chinese philosophy, language and culture; but since the Meiji Restoration in the late nineteenth century, Japan had begun to see China as an antiquated country. With the Westernisation of Japan, the Japanese saw China as losing out to the industrialised Western countries and began to weaken ties with it. My father had viewed this as betrayal of the utmost.

'We were married the year before the Japanese invasion,' my mother said softly, 'It took three days. There was a Christian ceremony where we were both dressed in white, and a tea pouring ceremony following a wedding banquet. It took two days to complete.'

'Did you wear the traditional *kua*?' I asked.

'It was long dress, made up of a tunic and skirt, extremely red, intricately embroidered with flowers, peony and lotus with birds and dragons in gold thread,' she added remembering in detail, 'it belonged to my mother.'

'What did you wear in your hair?' I asked.

'My mother had jasmine flowers woven into some of her gold combs, it was very pretty,' she said, pensively remembering everything.

'All dressed and serving tea, it must have been a very hot and long-winded ceremony?' I added insensitively.

'They were good moments because I knew how proud my father was; we survived very tearful minutes in between because I knew my life from then on would be changed forever. He looked at me with such soulful eyes, it was heart-breaking for such a happy occasion,' she said.

'Because you were there with him through that critical transitional period of his life?' I said pensively.

'As he was for me, but I was striking out for fresh fields and new pastures with marriage and children. I had often wished that I could have had more than those fifteen years together,' she said.

'A father's love can be unconditional and you had such exciting adventures too,' I said picturing them in the boat, huddled, with waves throwing them about.

His greatest gift to her was confidence which developed the assurance that even as a woman she could have ambitious dreams and fulfil them. Her sense of truth came from her heart, but what was in her heart came from her father. There were times when she would come home feeling that she was inferior because some plantation manager was rude to her. She would discuss this with her father and time after time, he guided her to think honestly, and not let small irritations grind her down. She mastered the difference between objectivity and subjectivity in essence, most of the lessons her father had learnt for himself. She understood his way of moving forwards. She spent most of her private time studying, reading and learning. By the time she was married she spoke two languages and three dialects of Chinese. She had also achieved her professional qualifications Being a scholar her father had taught her to be analytical and critical not only in reading books but also in everyday life.

Unfortunately her husband, my father, looked to a woman in a traditional Confucian way. He had hidden most of this from her during the months when he courted and wooed her. Despite the fact that she was bright, qualified and had a small personal income, he expected her to be a *yin* to his *yang*. The yin person would be described as soft, yielding, receptive, passive and tranquil. The yang man on the other hand, was hard, active, assertive and dominating. He did not envisage my mother not understanding that. She scorned the Confucian ethic in the poem from the *Book of Poetry* which read that 'Women should not take part in public affairs; they should be at home tending silkworms and weaving.'

There would be many altercations between them throughout their married life because he did not soften his chauvinistic attitude. Although she did not give me details, my mother would often blame this on a bad childhood where my father had been left by his parents and put in the care of aunts.

'I found out after a short time that he was rather cold emotionally,' she said that day as we went on to talk about marriage.

'Was that a hard thing to bear?' I asked.

'Yes. I am quite an emotional woman. And I wanted to be loved deeply. Thankfully I had so much to do. I was working towards the completion of my "normal" studies, I was teaching school until lunch. Also I had many friends and my father, who was getting very old,' she said.

'But dad was supposed to be wise, he was a teacher after all?' I asked.

'Yes he taught physics at the local English secondary school,' she explained, 'in that time they also sent some young qualified Englishman to teach biology. Needless to say, they did not get on.'

'That must have been difficult for you seeing that you got on with everyone despite the colour of their skin,' I interjected, knowing what she would say next.

'It was really frustrating I was trained by my father to talk to everyone, to be comfortable sitting in anyone's living room and to have dinner with the English, Chinese or Malay, regardless of race, it was tiresome to be made to feel that we were racially different in any way,' she explained.

She never quite understood why my father hated the English. He was good looking, well read and educated, someone who could have carried his head high. But somewhere in his psyche lay the sharp sting of unrequited honour and respect. A racial slur would be like arrow in the heart if one was not prepared for the differences in opinion between cultures. I began to understand that my father was unprepared as he came from a family where they hated the English because they felt that they were exploiting the other races. They were the governing class in the colonial era in Malaya and provided a well-organised administration of civil servants. Ingenuity was used to govern a country fast filling up with Malay immigrants from Indonesia joining the ethnic Malays, the Chinese, and the Indians from south India. The British resorted to the same divide-and-rule policy as they did in India. By and large, it worked quite well.

The British also had a pro-Malay policy because as colonial administrators; they were careful to develop a mutual trust with the Malay sultans. The other races did not seem to mind this. The Chinese were given the freedom to do business and trade. They were appreciative of the law and order created by the English so that they could prosper commercially. Rubber plantations, tin mines, and urban and rural commerce flourished because they were owned and run effectively by the Chinese. The Malays were free to farm in that countryside and owned small businesses in towns. Indians formed the backbone of the manual labouring class and the civil service. Overall, the creation of a solid infrastructure of transport, communications, education and health facilities by the British allowed the Malayan economy to flourish.

My mother had heard this explained to her by her father hundreds of times. He considered himself lucky to have arrived in this place, at the right time. They grew from being immigrants to the elite Chinese in Malaya because of his wealth, business acumen and crucially, his ability to understand his new homeland and their rulers. He also had a good command of the English language which helped to smooth business negotiations and explain the way out in difficult circumstances. He had the freedom to work hard and to continue to progress. The turmoil in China had desecrated these basic rights, but now having arrived at their 'brave new world,' they could begin to establish their lives and prosper again. The confidence he exuded influenced his daughter in a positive way.

My father would see his wife not only as someone who would continue to outshine him even as a woman because she was a person with an optimistic perspective of the world. In her eyes the opportunities to thrive were there, in front of her, to be picked up one by one. She would not waste her life with procrastination. She was enchanted by the new home he offered her. They lived in quarters provided by the civil service in Malaya for teaching staff and modelled like the ones the British had built in India. It was a four-bedroom bungalow with an inside kitchen and an outside one. This had wood and charcoal burning stoves which were used for making Chinese wok dishes and fiery Indian curries. There was a dining room, a living room, five bedrooms and four bathrooms. It stood on almost an acre of land and housed garages and rooms for the servants which were connected to the main house by covered walkways. It had standard English civil service furniture and my mother appreciated every armchair and dining table because it was different. She had some rattan and wicker chairs made to add some lightness to the heavy furniture which was built to last lifetimes.

Most of all she loved the garden enclosed within a hedge of ixora. There were shrubs and bushes of hibiscus, croton, jasmine, gardenias, bougainvillea and oleanders of vivid yellow. There were raised beds where there were rows upon rows of canna and the bird of paradise, the quintessential tropical flower. Just like a carpet to bring all these together there was a lawn of tough grass that withstood monsoon rains. A gardener who tended this, together with two other assistants, and who answered to the name Raj, orchestrated the watering, cutting, pruning, mowing, mulching and weeding. His favourite job was looking after the five fruit trees of mango and *rambutan*, a delicious tropical fruit that tasted like a lychee and had white, sweet and juicy flesh.

'Did you have fun living in such a big space?' I asked suddenly, not really believing that one could be so lucky.

'It was a dream garden. I spent a lot of my time propagating plants from cuttings Raj would bring me from other gardens. Mostly I tended a little orchid garden of Vanda orchids,' she said quickly. 'It was a good walk going round through the garden, which I did mostly in the evenings, always feeling so privileged having a gardener to do all the hard work. There were countless beds of these exotic white, mauve, lilac and pale pink Vanda and cattleya flowers.'

'What a good life it must have been mama, fulfilling your job as a teacher, having such a beautiful garden and still able, from time to time, to visit granddad,' I said.

'Yes it was and I will treasure those years always,' she said, with tears in her eyes.

This idyllic lifestyle would soon be brutally interrupted. The invading force of the Japanese army would literally come marching through, trampling the flowers and crushing the peace of the gardens, hearts, minds, bodies and souls.

CHAPTER EIGHT

A Time Of War

The Japanese occupied Malaya from December 1941 to 1945. There was no peace for the local citizens during that entire period of almost four years. The beautiful house with the lotus ponds and my parents' home with hedgerows of ixora were commandeered by its military forces and all local inhabitants turned out into the streets.

Fortunately my mother and father, foreseeing all this, had already escaped with the family to a property in Sitiawan, on the Perak coast about sixty miles away. It was close to one of the estates, secluded from the main highways which they thought the Japanese army would take. Most of the members of the family had driven there in convoy, taking with them necessary items, clothing, medicine and food. They brought three of their most faithful amahs. The two rubber plantations had ceased operations and all the labourers were sent home to fend for themselves and help their families flee from the invading military force. It was an unsettling and fearful time for everyone. My mother spent her evenings comforting her father. She would read him the familiar stories he loved from the same books he had brought from China. Her voice calmed him down and as she looked at him from the glow of the kerosene lamps they used in the evenings, she could see that he was comfortable. She managed with her composure to obliterate the war raging around them and bring serenity to his sparsely decorated bedroom. His world had collapsed, but he gained solace in hearing her daughter's voice telling him about the days when heroines were kind and beautiful and heroes were strong men who fought and loved. She read many poems from the Tang poet Li Bai who wrote in that exquisite minimalist way about love

> *'To sail off in a skiff I was about*
> *Suddenly I heard singing ashore all out,*
> *A thousand feet deep Pearl Bloom Lake may be*
> *Compare not it could to Wang's love for me.'*

As my mother recited these words there were tears in her eyes. She remembered what a strong man her father was but the trauma of the war had taken its toll on him. He was aware that his sons were out on their own and had the means to look after themselves. They had from time to time brought back horrific stories of the cruelty of the invaders. Two of them had been shot by the Japanese in Singapore. The Japanese were brutal, men without mercy for prisoners and thus without the humanity. For those who were not from that nation it was something that could never be understood.

'Apart from my husband, my father was the only other man in the household during the Japanese occupation,' my mother said quietly.

'That was quite a responsibility and how many of you were there?' I asked.

'There were twelve to fourteen of us including the three servants,' she said.

'Were you afraid?' I asked. 'After all, the Japanese were well known for their disrespect and often raped women who were not Japanese.'

'We were told by my father to look as ugly and as old as we could, so we would dye our hair grey and smudge our faces with black charcoal,' she answered.

'How terrible,' I said.

'Do you know, it was not always bad because I learnt so much,' she said calmly.

Her sister had trained as a nurse before the war and it was through her that my mother learnt basic nursing. She also learnt how to administer injections. These simple procedures would turn out to be useful throughout the war. One such times was when she had to go to Singapore to visit her brother who was working for the British. She was too late because before she got to the city, he had already been captured by the Japanese and shot. On hearing the news, she immediately turned around and took the first train back to Sitiawan. Her father, now a devout Christian had taught her to pray and she remembered praying in the railway station in Singapore. She got on the train and when it was traveling through Johor state it was bombed. To her amazement her carriage was the only one which was not hit in the carnage. When she got out there were many wounded passengers. She maintained the composure of a nurse and helped the wounded. There was smoke and wailing everywhere but she remained very calm, a practice she had mastered. She would remember that day for the rest of her life, convinced that God had delivered her from death and injury.

'I was sitting in the carriage and I could hear the train being bombed,' my mother said calmly, one day when we talked about God. 'It happened so fast, there is just all the noise and everything shaking.'

'What did you do, I mean what were your first reactions?' I asked loudly.

'I just fell to the ground and tried to hide under the table, there was so much screaming,' she said.

'I am sure that you were scared, what happened next?' I said.

'The train came to a screeching stop, there was more noise and then quiet, but there was smoke everywhere. I got up just grabbed my bag, opened the door and jumped off.' she said, closing her eyes as if to picture the moment.

'So you landed on a field or something?' I said.

'Yes it was open and cultivated. I think an abandoned rice field, a paddy field. My heart was thumping so hard, like it would be if you thought you were going to die,' she said.

'Yes, I can imagine how horrific that would be, I would be terrified,' I answered.

'The whole train seemed to be burning and everywhere there was shouting, yelling and sobbing. When I fell to the ground with just my handbag, first I was astonished I could stand up again, she said quickly, 'I looked at my train carriage and realised that it was the only one which was not bombed.'

'What?!' I replied, 'how did that happen?

'It was a long train, meaning there were many carriages I was in the middle coach and the train was snaking round a bend and the planes just missed. For me it was Divine mercy and from then on, I became a devout Christian,' she answered softly.

It was a very moving moment. There were other instances of her life which I will remember as vividly but nothing that would get my heart racing as this story. For her this moment on a paddy field alone, amidst an inferno of burning train coaches and the human suffering of the injured and the dead; she experienced her own miracle of salvation.

There was another instance when the Japanese were doing house to house checks. My mother was pregnant and she opened the door. The Japanese officer raced in checking room by room, upending tables and chairs as he searched for any evidence of cohesion or solidarity with the English or Australian forces which were now put in prisoner-of-war camps. There was a resistance army fighting against the Japanese during the war, and they were made up mainly of Chinese. In the bedroom my mother remembered to her horror that she had kept a photo of an English doctor in the full uniform of an army major, Royal Engineers. Thankfully the Japanese officer did not see the photo as it fell to the floor. After that incident all photos were burnt just in case these soldiers returned.

The greatest joy of both my parents was the cultivation of a farm. The skills that she had gained from the rubber tappers in the plantation were now applied to running a farm where she grew sweet potatoes, tapioca, corn, beans, green leafy kale, onions, chillies, garlic, ginger and cultivated fruit trees producing mangoes, custard apples, papaya and bananas. She learnt how to collect rainwater for the crops. She raised chickens buying the first few chicks from a Malay farmer and fenced them in a little compound near the house so that her father could collect the eggs. They were producing so many eggs that of these were exchanged for rice which a nearby farmer was growing in irrigated paddy fields. As they were close to the sea, they could buy fish cheaply from the local fisherman. There was bream, grouper, mackerel, snapper and moonfish, there were clams and cockles; these were fished in abundance from the Straits of Malacca, the sea which lay not quite ten miles from the farm. My mother learnt how to pickle and preserve vegetables such as radishes, ginger and also green kale. They also mastered the technique of producing dried salted fish, which was mainly from giant mackerel cut into chunks breadthwise, which was called *ikan tenggiri* in Malay. Fried salted dried fish was one of the great side dishes on my mother's dinner table, a great compliment to some of the pork and vegetables dishes. Even during the war she had not learnt to cook leaving that to her father's trusted *Ah-Ling*.

'I ran the farm like clockwork and knew exactly when and where each crop had to be planted. Thankfully we had some of our labourers from the plantation who found me during the war,' my mother said thoughtfully.

'Did you do everything or was there a division of labour?' I asked, quite unable to picture my mother on a farm.

'It was all trial and error but you learnt fast when you are hungry. I started out with a vegetable patch but soon found I could grow sweet potatoes, yams and tapioca easily. Those were during the days when we did not find a rice farmer yet,' she said, not really answering my question.

'I am sure you were content to be alive,' I said interrupting her account.

'It was such a different life, but there was so much to do and yes, it was such an adventure,' she said contently.

'There must have many around you willing to help with the planting, the all-round care, and the harvesting,' I said seeing the whole picture.

'Yes, your father was very supportive even though he did not know planting the way I understood it. I figured out the soil, the weather and how delicate vegetables can be with snails!' she said smiling.

That was the side of my mother I dearly loved. She always remained optimistic when danger surrounded her. Her fearless determination created that well-rounded and positive person.

I think she tried so hard to be the strong person her father had willed her to be. They remained very close during those days of war. She had less time for him because she had the farm, a husband and a son, my brother, already a year old. But she never let a night go by without coming into his bedroom to talk and pray. Towards the end of the war he became very frail. This deterioration began when his wife died in her sleep. She was a very beautiful woman and had been born in the city of Suzhou. She was always impeccably dressed and had an aristocratic bearing, with a lineage which could be traced back to the Emperor Qianglong.

She saw my grandfather for the first time and fell instantly in love in a garden, one of the many classic gardens in Suzhou, named Tiger Hill, where she was visiting with her fourth aunt. He happened to be there, a last-minute invitation by his uncle who lived in Shanghai. Amidst the azaleas, narcissus, tulips and water lilies, they could barely take their eyes off each other when introduced. However, she had a ceremonious bearing because she was not formally educated and was brought up in a cloistered world of women. He found that she could not share his innermost thoughts and emotions about China because she was always surrounded by her sisters and maids. She had a reticence, an aloofness, which he tried to explain to himself, that was a part of the female character. Nevertheless, there was an attraction because when they were alone together, she was an enchanting woman. The differences between them grew when they left China, mainly because she did not want to leave her family and homeland. He had really failed to convince her that the country was imploding, and that their lives along with their children's, were dangerously at stake.

'I think that was why he became close to me,' said my mother out of the blue.

'Because he was lonely and needed someone to talk to,' I replied.

'He was embarking on such a huge project and he probably discussed it with only a few of his friends. There was also the need to be secretive. I was there so young but gung ho about everything. I really gave him my total support. This planned voyage, the big escape from China simply captured my imagination,' she continued. 'The more he told me the more fascinated I became.'

'To the extent you became his partner in crime,' I said

'Yes his partner in exile who understood why he felt he had to leave.' she added. 'But my mama achieved some measure of peace at the end, especially in the house with the lotus ponds in Taiping.'

'What was her name?' I asked.

'She was named Wang Hui-Yin which means "great fame" in Chinese, said my mother quietly, 'and she was buried in the Christian Cemetery in Taiping.'

'Did you know her well?' I asked.

'No, but I respected and loved her. I was always with my father but she had her maids and my sisters…they were closer to her,' she answered, smiling knowingly.

Her grave was a simple memorial cross carved out of granite and an accompanying memorial plaque with her name carved out of the same stone and a simple message in Chinese, 'Devoted mother and beloved wife.' Her grave was looked after lovingly. Almost once a month for the rest of his life, he made sure that a small bouquet of tuberose, her favourite flower, was put under the cross.

CHAPTER NINE

Time Of Peace

My mother was a still young woman when the Japanese occupation of Malaya came to an end. She was also a mother of two, a son and daughter. Eager to forget the trauma of war, she visited her father's plantations which were in a state of ruin and overgrown with weeds and *lallang*, the tall grass that grew in the tropics. About half the labourers were still living there. They had survived mainly because they managed to grow sweet potatoes and tapioca, along with green vegetables, the local kale and cabbages and kept chickens which were previously hidden from the Japanese soldiers. Fortunately many of those who had lived through the war were mainly tappers. Within months they managed to get some of the estate working again. Supplies trickled in from the main towns but the process of restoration was slow because many of the roads to the plantations had to be rebuilt. Their homes were repaired and when word got round, new workers appeared eager to work again. The main house where the manager lived was renovated. It was a predominantly made of teak and it was difficult to find new sources of that particular hardwood. The jungle especially close to towns had been chopped down by the Japanese and the rich wood exported to Japan.

It took a longer time to mend hearts and minds. Many of the laborers had endured the hardships of war. They had hidden in caves, some had been captured by the Japanese and tortured. Some had been prisoners of war. The cultural norm was that families looked after their own. Gradually because of the increasing price of rubber and a general return to civil society, the atrocities of war dimmed. However the political situation had been in a state of flux since the end of the war against Japan. Some Chinese immigrants who had fought the war alongside the British but were not given the same rights as the Malays, started a rebellion against the British administration.

'It was called the war of the running dogs,' said my mother.

'Why running dogs?' I asked.

'It was a contemptuous term for those in Malaya who remained loyal to the British after the Second World War,' she replied.

'From whom, I mean who spread the idea?' I asked astutely.

'The Malayans who were ideologically communist and sympathetic to China even though China was only one-third communist then. The pro-Chinese anti-British idea was largely fuelled by an American senator named McCarthy,' my mother replied slowly.

'So it was out of one war and into another?' I said hurriedly, vaguely understanding and glossing over what the Americans had thought of communism in Asia.

'Most of the fighting was done in the jungle and areas around it, which included the mountainous forest and foothills running down the core of the peninsula for some three hundred miles,' she answered explicitly.

Soberly she continued to explain that afterwards the country was launched tumultuously into a period known as the Malayan emergency, where there was a twelve-year conflict between communist guerrillas, who called themselves the Malayan National Liberation Army (MNLA) and the British and Commonwealth forces. The MNLA had initially aided the English army defence against the Japanese during the Second World War. When it was over the group, mainly represented by the Chinese communist party wanted to be one of the parties considered for the future government of the country. This was staunchly refused by the British administration. So they established in a series of jungle bases and raided colonial police and military installations. Tin mines and rubber plantations were also frequent targets of communist bandit attacks. The idea was to destabilise the existing British government and make the colonial occupation of Malaya too expensive for the English to maintain.

This also meant that the civilian population was not spared. Those living on the fringes of the jungle were threatened with their lives if they refused to give food to the guerrillas. Travel between towns was disrupted and there was fear and distrust in the big towns. The British had to use ingenuity to fight the war because at its height there were some 8000 British soldiers fighting an army of approximately 40,000 men. It was hardly an even playing field. Also it was difficult to tell the difference between the loyal Chinese civilians and those hostile to the British, even though the established Chinese and Malays had shown their support from the start.

She went on to describe how the English devised the radical Briggs Plan. It relocated over a quarter of the population into 'new villages'. These were surrounded by barbed wire, police posts and floodlit in the dark. They were destined to keep the inhabitants in and the bandits out. Mostly, it was a means of ensuring that supplies of food were not leaked to the jungle guerrillas who could not sustain themselves without vital supplies.

'I find that strange in that there were communist supporters from the Chinese population who had fled from China,' I said.

'Yes but this was almost a new generation who were impoverished by the war and disillusioned by their lives under British rule,' she answered.

'They were in a minority but intent on creating disruption to law and order or to peace through discontent,' I said simply.

'And with no respect for what the first generation of Chinese like my father had actually done for the country. We were the people who took risks, built the towns, cleared the jungle and produced crops,' she said emotionally.

'Yes you were the generation who shed the tears and toiled and enabled the toiling masses,' I said understandably.

'What Confucius said about the three ways of attaining wisdom I do agree: first by reflection which is the noblest, second by imitation which is the easiest and third by experience which is the most bitter. I think he meant the most difficult,' she said.

'And I guess your father used all three methods to understand the political situation and carry on developing his estates in Malaya,' I answered not really understanding Confucius completely.

'Yes, the most difficult part about establishing yourself in a new country, and a new industry, rubber planting; was that one had to learn everything the hard way. Thankfully he had some business acumen!' she answered.

'Did the bandits stir up trouble in the plantations?' I asked.

'Yes it was mainly terrorism; often they would attack or worse, kill the local staff working for the planters,' she said

'You had mentioned cooks or serving staff,' I answered.

'This was done mainly to scare the planters, often to raid the well-stocked larders which they knew we had, in the main house,' she replied.

It is very difficult to forget those conversations with my mother. She breathed life in describing those bleak years of the emergency by emotionally explaining in detail. The Briggs plan forbade all food in cars whilst traveling between towns in case these were hijacked by bandits on the highway. She described how it was nearly impossible to travel between cities without food of any kind. That disrupted the culture of food the Malayans were already developing before the war. It was considered kind to bring presents of food when visiting, whether it was baskets of fruit, baked cakes or cookies, even fully cooked meals.

'We could not pack picnics to enjoy during our long car journeys,' she said.

'Or have all that lovely fruit picked in the estate brought to you when the manager visited your father,' I replied.

'We had a lovely mango plantation, but it became impossible to transport the fruits,' she added ruefully.

She also went on to pitch the idea that the war of the running dogs, gave the local Malay, Chinese and Indian population a chance to develop a trust in the British colonial government because they were fighting a common enemy. This encouraged the English effort and spearheaded by a certain British high commissioner named General Gerald Templer, turned the tide of the war by adopting the policy that the British had to win the hearts and minds of the local population in order to win the war. This was achieved in part by giving the Malays and the jungle tribespeople medical and food aid if they helped fight the communist bandits. This drew the guerrillas deeper into the jungle and denied them of essential resources, mainly food.

Simultaneously in towns Templer gave the Chinese the right to vote and critical land rights, thereby sealing their loyalties to the country. The British led by Templar succeeded in overthrowing communist political ambitions against the colonial administration. The emergency is often portrayed as a Malay struggle against the communists. In fact it included a huge Chinese and Indian initiative, especially those living in the countryside from the new villages and plantations.

'When the war of the running dogs ended, the local population, though mainly made up of immigrants began to look at the country as theirs. They were proud of their contribution which led to the success of the economy,' she said.

'But also their massive support to the British in the war effort,' I finished.

'Mind you, the British were superb in building the infrastructure of roads, railways, and communications,' she continued.

'They probably saw Malaya as a critical hub in their empire,' I added more sarcastically.

'My husband Meng-Hua saw everything on a more personal level, he always felt that there was some racial prejudice involved because the English were granted more privileges,' she said.

'While you felt he opposite, that everyone deserved their day in the sun because of hard work, imagination and clever thinking,' I replied.

'It was difficult even for my father, a Chinese Mandarin, to imagine how a small island nation, England, could win an empire.' she said finally.

'But all ambitions come to an end as we saw how difficult it was for the English to survive after the war,' I said.

Agreeing with what I said, she went on to explain how even during the Emergency, hard diplomatic talks were held for the independence of the Federation of Malaya which comprised the nine Malay states and the two British Straits Settlements of Penang and Malacca. The 'straits' always referred to the Straits of Malacca, a narrow stretch of water between the Malay peninsula and Sumatra which strategically connected the Indian Ocean with the Pacific, thus making it one of the most important shipping lanes in the world. The Federation of Malaya became independent of British colonial rule in 1957. The Federation was headed by a British High Commissioner who took orders from the Federation's Executive and Legislative councils. There was also a Malay Conference of rulers comprising the nine sultans and they had power to oversee Muslim citizens in Islamic matters. In rotation they would elect a king or the Yang di-Pertuan Agong, who held this austere position for five years. Overall British law prevailed.

'But the Chinese had very little control on government?!' I said astonished.

'Yes the Malays call themselves "bumiputras" which I think means princes of the soil,' she said.

'It must have been hard for the Chinese, being second class citizens,' I replied.

'No strangely the Chinese were just glad to be given the freedom to do business. Certainly my father was. He was also pleased to be governed by English law,' she said quietly.

She also talked of how her father knew that once, the idea of feudal China and the rule of emperors was of great importance. By the time he left, the Mandate of Heaven, as he remembered it, was no more. What was evolving was a better system, described in one word, democracy. I could see how she was full of admiration for the mind of the man who not only steered the boat out of China, but also knew how to manoeuvre in a world that was changing rapidly. He spoke to her frequently of his understanding of the ethos of his freedom, which included the opportunity for prosperity and personal success.

The idea of leaving China meant leaving a past that stagnated in ideas which brought no further philosophical or economic progress. He found himself drawn to the ideas of west. He had read the novels of American writers including John Steinbeck and was astonished. They inspired ideas of citizens being able to grow to their fullest potential unhampered by barriers. In older civilisations like China these had been erected to maintain the class system of the emperors and Mandarins. He was himself a Mandarin but considered his role outdated and simply, outclassed.

'He had a very humble attitude because he felt that there was so much to learn,' my mother said.

'In all aspects probably. I am sure he was very pleased that he was no longer in charge of decisions concerning the governing of the place,' I replied.

'I think he was successful because he learnt hard and so well,' she said.

'He was totally ready for all the changes that were to confront him, he was a rich man but he was also an intelligent citizen,' I answered.

His new life required so many risk-taking investment decisions that he was grateful that the new country he found himself in was properly and democratically governed. He kept ideas of supremacy and colonialism to himself. This maintained the balance he had fought so hard to manage in his mind. He knew it as 'chi', the life force that flows through your body to give it an energy for life. There had to be good 'chi' in order to live a life and harmoniously achieve peace. He believed that in order to have peace there had to be respect. The idea of respect or *xiao shun* was central to Confucian thought. He was content that a large part of Confucius's idea of virtue so firmly ingrained in his mind, was now unfolding in his family and gradually in the country he now lived.

CHAPTER TEN

Lessons For Women

My mother often told me that her father's wisdom and wealth 'afforded her education'. I knew what she meant.

In those days rich men simply wished to see their young daughters married off to wealthy men. But her father recognised her emotional and natural intelligence from a young age and was determined to develop that. He began by teaching her himself. He respected smart women. One of his favourite heroines was the philosopher Ban Zhao from the Han dynasty. She was known to be a multifaceted scholar but renowned as a co-author of the *Book of the Han*, which recorded the history of the western Han Dynasty. There were over a hundred volumes written by men before her but she took over, and wrote the last eight volumes. They were historical and chronological accounts of emperors, nobles and officials including biographies of important people. Included in these sagas were also essays in law, arts, literature and astronomy. But Ban Zhao was best remembered as the author of *Lessons for Women*, a treatise on etiquette and behaviour for all the women in court, mostly educated women.

'Imagine that! A book for women like *Debrett's*, on manners and etiquette in court,' my mother explained.

'It's unimaginable to think that the Chinese were so civilised so long ago,' I replied.

'But as a woman I have always asserted that they were not as civilised as I would have liked because Confucian ethics repressed women and woman's rights for centuries,' she said.

I was mesmerised by what followed. Ban Zhao gave long and interesting accounts, often interspersed by personal stories about how badly women were treated in ancient China. She began with a poem written before the Ming period:

'How sad it is to be a woman
Nothing on earth is so cheap
Boys are like gods fallen from heaven
Their hearts brave the Four Oceans
The wind and dust of a thousand miles

No one is glad when a girl is born
By her the family sets no store
When she grows up she hides in her room
Afraid to look a man in the face....'

Mama looked as if it was not worth repeating because she was annoyed that filial piety in Confucian China produced such meek and scared women, who knew that their lives was going to be limited from childhood. The wants, dreams and desires of young girls did not matter. The family was the only critical element of their lives. It began with service to the family, then the emperor and the state. A woman's life was completed with an impersonal establishment of her own personality as dictated by society. It was a harsh fate.

Parents were in charge of their children's marriage. Usually marriages were arranged. If a woman or girl refused to marry she could be forced into becoming a concubine or prostitute. Women were not allowed to have conversations with men. They had little chance anyway, as they were confined to the house or compound where their parents lived. They were regarded as burdens because they were unable to work ordinarily, to farm, or even go to war as soldiers. The only way a girl was able to gain the respect of the family or community was to perform her biological function to have sons and thus continue the family name.

My mother then proceeded to tell me that filial piety demanded that a girl had to remain chaste until she was married. The Chinese did not believe in marriage because there was love or a strong bond. Marriage was for the social enhancement of status and to unite the names of two families so that all would benefit from the enhanced financial prospects and the growth in family lineage. If her husband should die before her, she would remain a widow and keep her new chastity. My mother then told me that the Ming dynasty probably had the highest suicide rates in Chinese history due to women abiding by chastity laws. It was a very sombre account of the some of the stricter aspects of the culture and so much less joyful than her accounts of concubines and courtesans. She had me imagine that if I had lived in Ming dynasty I would have preferred to be one of those elite courtesans who were dressed in beautiful red silks, who wrote and played music on the zither. It was a string instrument which comprised of seven silk strings tautly laid on a shallow box.

'You would have had to wear turtle shell nails to pluck on the zither,' she said to me.

'How fabulous! That and making music would have been a far better choice than being a rich Chinese man's wife,' I said with a laugh.

'Yes I couldn't agree with you more,' she said laughing with me.

She continued in a more serious vein to reminisce on how lucky she was to have escaped the entrapment a traditional Chinese union would have brought. She was a beautiful girl and her father had said that more than five families had asked for her hand in marriage to one of their sons. She was also very sensitive to all the physical aspects of being a wife. She could not imagine making love to a man who she did not love, let alone one who was too old, too clumsy or too ugly.

Since she was fifteen she had fantasised her future husband. Her mother had told her in no uncertain terms that her purity was all important. She was encouraged to remain a virgin in order to present to her husband, a 'flawless piece of jade'. Very little is written about women's roles in a Chinese court of the emperor and his mandarins. But accounts of male masculinity are highly portrayed in the Ming and Qing dynasty classic novels such as *The Water Margin*, *The Peony Pavilion* and *The Dream of the Red Chamber*. My mother was often outraged that women were rarely honored in Chinese literature.

'Even in our most famous novel *The Dream of the Red Chamber*,' she said carefully, 'the protagonist was a man.'

'Of course, what did you expect?' I interrupted. 'It was a semi-autobiographical story of the great writer Cao Xueqin who lived in eighteenth century China.'

'And a memorial to all the women he had known from his youth; his friends, relatives and servants,' she answered, 'but he rarely praised them.'

We often had long discussions about themes in the Chinese classics. My mother was well versed on the ideas of allegories. She was totally captured by the idea of a story within a story. She also revelled in riddles, puzzles and any small idea that made her think. The idea of lineage made her think of finding a place for the complexity of family dynamics within the larger demands of society. Mostly, she wondered about keeping Chinese traditions alongside adopting the best that Western culture could offer. Her father had often taught her that nothing she had read of the Chinese classics would be lost in her new life outside China, if she remembered the core concepts.

She talked about the book *The Dream of the Red Chamber* with aplomb as though she knew every single angle of it. Loving the allegory, she described it's meaning as red dust or the stone; often coming back to the novel's two themes, that of romantic love and the transient nature of earthly material values.

'So was it basically a treatise of Taoist, Confucian and Buddhist values?' I asked simply.

'Yes, but what makes it one of the monuments of literature was that it attempted to describe Chinese culture in family terms,' she answered. 'It was an immense piece of writing that was based on moral and spiritual values.'

'I am sure that was what grandfather taught you since you were very young,' I replied.

'It was difficult to understand ideas like red dust at first, but then my father explained to me the Buddhist belief that the whole world is red dust…' she paused, '… a mere illusion and thus to be shunned.'

She went on to explain that the stone was the protagonist and hero Jia Baoyu. What was so imaginative in the allegory was that in the dream vision Jia was indeed a stone reborn as a prince. Contrary to the realm in which life imitates art, the story goes on to propose the idea that the world is only a dream from which we must awaken. The Buddhist idea was that one had to understand that finding enlightenment in the world was an impossible dream. I did not fully understand the profoundness of our talk. Much later in my life I recalled how well it matched Greek philosophy.

The curious fact was that Chinese women were admired for both their femininity and their strength. *The Dream of the Red Chamber* suggests that women were in essence as pure as spring water whereas men were as impure as mud. The feminine traits of Chinese women were largely purity, spirituality, sincerity and intelligence. However as the author was a man, my mother had her own opinions and was often critical about the story.

'I just never really understood what the dream was all about,' she said suddenly.

'Did you discuss this with grandfather?' I asked simply.

'Yes,' she answered 'and he told me that there could have been two dreams.'

'What a major and a minor dream?' I said tritely.

The big dream was in the form of the allegory where Jia Baoyu has an afternoon nap in a chamber, where he dreams of encountering the Goddess of Disenchantment who instructs him to save his family of honourable ancestors from descending into ruin. Then he is led into a bedchamber where he meets a young girl named Precious Virtue. They make love, which is described in the book as 'a sport of cloud and rain.' When Jia wakes up from this he is led into the real world. This is where his life of unrequited love and other dramas begin. The story of the Red Chamber or Hung Lou Meng , also symbolised the rooms where the daughters of wealthy families lived and where they dreamt the dreams of young women. They were often of the perfect life with the ideal husband who would rescue them from whatever they needed to be saved. These were women who conformed to life but were seething with frustration in a world which did not fulfil them. The book has many proverbs. My mother drew on one which I remembered well and it read, *'when the unreal is taken for the real, the real becomes the unreal.'*

There have been many debates on the truth behind this saying from Hung Lou Meng. Essentially my mother interpreted it as meaning that each individual was responsible as a creator of their own thoughts. She also drew lessons for women from this, often ambitiously, to think that they should be educated and thus not have to depend on men to redeem them. Thus they were able to see for themselves what it required to lead their lives. It followed that they should not be prevailed upon to marry if they did not love their husbands.

'So the minor dream in the book was represented by all the dreams young women dreamt from their red chambers or bedrooms?' I said.

'Yes and in accordance with the title of the book,' my mother replied.

'But all this is fiction,' I said, 'who were the strong women in China as Mao Zedong indicated when he said women held up half the world.'

'They possessed the qualities as strong men did,' she replied, 'they were strong in action, mainly in the military; showed great intellect and were often victorious when the odds were stacked against them.'

'Indeed those are great qualities,' I replied 'and granddad was always in awe of alpha women.'

'He was fascinated by them,' she continued, 'he would tell me stories of Western women who would become heroines because they nursed the sick, or invented some important medicine. There were others who led armies to battle and the Queen who led an Empire.'

'Yes let me think,' I said, 'that would be Florence Nightingale, Marie Curie, Joan of Arc and Queen Victoria.'

We often reverted to the book *Lessons for Women*.

As her father had taught her, she instilled in me that the one most important role of a woman was to understand how crucial we were in society. The book gently advises women to be generously compliant and respectful towards the greater purpose of familial harmony. The service of women in this regard was considered to be an important cornerstone of Chinese family life. The family unit was an integral part of Chinese culture. It sustained it and gave it longevity. These crucial links later became the founding text in Confucius's work on feminism.

'You see how important women were even in those early days of the Han dynasty?' said my mother. 'They did hold up the world.'

'Ban Zhao must have been very confident in her thinking and intellect,' I replied complacently.

Enthusiastically mother continued to tell me that she was called on to teach the Empress Deng Sui, the members of the court, and eventually the Emperor Shang of the Han. Zhao worked from the royal library which was her domain and was given the title, the Gifted One. She edited the *Biographies of Eminent Women* written by Lu Xiang and meticulously supervised the copying of texts from bamboo slips and silk onto newly invented scrolls of paper.

'When my father talked about her body of work, he was in fervent awe thinking of all the calligraphy that went into writing out those early Chinese books,' said my mother enthusiastically.

'I guess the brushes were made of lotus leaf and flowers,' I added simply.

'Yes and the ink was made of soot, animal glue sometimes with incense and medicinal scents added,' she replied.

'How fabulously exotic those times seem now, mama,' I finished.

It was only the beginning of her accounts, she saved the military heroines for another day, prolonging the excited inquisitiveness she had evoked in me. I loved the way she recalled history. When she talked about Ping Yang, she would say that without this ubiquitous princess we might not have had a Tang Dynasty, which is always to be remembered as the Golden Age of Imperial China.

Ping was outstanding because as the daughter of the nobleman Li Yuan, she also fought shoulder to shoulder with him in drawn out battles against the Sui. These victories united vast areas of the northern and southern China. When she died, she was given a military funeral much to the disgust of the chauvinist men in the imperial army.

'In much the same way there was also the woman soldier Wu Zetian who fought behind the Emperor Taizong and his son Li Zhi,' she said.

'Yes and she was made an emperor,' I said.

'The only one who had to fight her way to victory and fame,' she answered rapidly.

'Yes and I remember grandfather talking at length about those Tang cavalry victories which helped extend China's western boundaries into Central Asia,' I added excitedly. 'Where would China be without that and Tibet beyond?'

'A smaller and poorer country,' she replied, 'and much more mediocre in culture and tradition.'

She spoke enthusiastically of the warrior heroines from the Ming Dynasty especially of the fabled Lin Siniang who fought for her king by training an army of women. Duly impressed, King Zhu fell in love with her, married her and made her a princess.

'Enough has been said about Hua Mulan from the northern Wei Dynasty,' my mother said quietly, 'but it was no mean feat to fight in place of your father and for twelve years, disguised as a man.'

'Yes,' I replied, 'taking the place of her swordsman father, using his sword.'

'So much a part of a woman's idea of service for the honour of the family,' mama said knowingly, 'but I also imagine she loved the adventure of it.'

'Legend has it that she was enthralled, riding from the Yellow River to the Black Mountains,' I replied, 'in north-eastern China.'

'Yes apart from her fighting skills, her name Mulan was quite a masculine name,' said mama, 'much like mine, before I changed it.'

We progressed and finally talked at length about the poet polymath Wang Zhenyi from the Qing period.

'How inspirational it must be if your grandfather was an astronomer, his wife a poet and between them they produced a son, your father, who became a mathematician,' she said in wonder.

'And who also had a great love of geography,' I said, 'I would enjoy the conversations across the dining table!'

'First, you had to be very bright, because there were a lot of books to read!' she said.

As science and mathematics ran in the Wang family. I was not amazed that such an intellectual lineage would have produced the prolific Zhenyi. Her academic granddad Wang Zeifu was the governor of a county near Nanjing, but spent his life reading books which he collected in seventy-five bookshelves. Being close to him, Zhenyi read most of them too, including Euclid's *Elements*. She wrote among other books, the *Simple Elements of Calculation*.

Mathematics aside, Wang's other books were mostly on subjects concerning women, especially on the subject of inequality between the sexes. My mother was inspired by her longer poems, often quoting from it.

'So important is the doorway
Occupying the throat of the mountain
Looking down from heaven
The sun sees the yellow river streaming,
It's made to believe
That women are the same as men,
Why then are you not convinced
That daughters can be heroic?'

When Zhenyi's innovative grandfather died, the family moved to Jilin near the Great Wall of China to be close to where they imagined laid his spirit of patriotism. There, in her fifties she learnt horse riding, archery and the martial arts from Aa, the wife of a Mongolian general. She led an inspired life. It was the sort of life which has captured my mother's imagination.

Mama was not content to live the cloistered life of a mandarin's granddaughter but in her youth, longed for a life of adventure not unlike like Ching Shito, a woman pirate who commandeered a fleet of 300 boats manned by several thousand men. She even imagined the freedom of being the legendary Ng Mui, the founder of Chinese martial arts at the Shaolin temple. Mui developed the 'white crane' method and 'the dragon' style art of fighting and spent her life training for the strength and fluidity of her body. These were stories that motivated countless Chinese women, including my mother.

'Life is simply like art. You need the imagination and the courage to pursue, finally to create.' my mother said after her long discourses on the women in ancient China.

'Yes and if one adds two plus two and it always equals four, we will never get there,' I said without thinking.

'Yes because imagination makes us fly,' she said, 'the moment you doubt you can fly, you cease forever to be able to do it.'

'I love that quote mama,' I ended. 'And I know from where it came.'

CHAPTER ELEVEN

Yellow Mountain

If you are planning for a year, sow seeds
If you are planning for a decade, plant trees
If you are planning for a lifetime, educate people

(Chinese proverb)

After the Second World War, my mother's family which consisted of her father and six unmarried siblings well into their fifties, returned to the house by the lotus ponds. They would live there for the next twenty years. It took five years but the house and its ponds were rebuilt and restored to its pre-war glory. My grandfather was in his nineties. He was elegant, walking slowly without a stick, and in possession of a mind that was still razor sharp. He loved looking up at the Maxwell peaks from his back garden, often reminiscing on how they reminded him of the Yellow Mountains in Anhui.

'I would often sit with him and talk about the time when he was young,' my mother would say.

'Did you leave papa on his own?' I asked.

'Yes, your papa was the principal of a school in another town. He was given a small house which came almost completely with a previously hired housekeeper. I thought it was not the best idea to move you and Yang to a new school. Your brother had to be monitored because he did not take his studies seriously.' she replied.

'Yes I remember his passion for building little model planes and attempting to fly them in the garden,' I said.

'He would spend hours in his room too,' she said 'in the end we had to get him a private tutor who disciplined him into becoming quite a good student who achieved high marks in school.'

I knew she was talking about my brother Yang, whom I loved dearly. He was a reclusive young man who had ambitions of being a great mechanical engineer one day, working for Rolls Royce or some other huge conglomerate. My mother always realised the he would, given time, land on his feet. Apart from being with her children, she chose to be with her father more than her husband. She wanted to bring her father back to the town which had literally meant the world to him after he had made the decision to leave China. She was grateful and impressed that here in a foreign country he had completed his life's work of providing well for his wife and children. He was never away from his books which kept his spirit alive. He had missed China but in that house with the lotus ponds, on the foothills of the Main Range of Malaya, he was at peace with himself. He did not find it difficult to be thankful that he was given not only another chance at life, but also another view of mountains not unlike his beloved Yellow Mountain.

He was also aware that his daughter was progressing really well her own career. By now she was the headmistress of a small but growing primary school run by Christian missionaries in that little idyllic town at the foot of the Maxwell peaks. When traveling with her father in search of a new home during those years of uncertainty and upheaval, she loved Taiping the moment she saw it. Nestled at the foothills of the Maxwell Hills, it looked secure and beautifully lush. The mist from the hills would settle like a thin veil over the lakes in the morning light. She thought this was magical. My mother also liked the name Taiping. It was quite unlike many of the towns with harsh unpronounceable names, which they had driven past down the peninsula of Malaya, decades ago.

Malaya seemed like a huge, fearful and an unknown territory to a Chinese family unfamiliar with their new homeland. Having travelled almost seven thousand miles by sea and land, and suddenly chancing on this green, picturesque town which looked like somewhere they could establish a new home, seemed blissful. She knew it the moment she set eyes on it. She remembered how it took little persuasion for her father to say he agreed. This also had the promise of a place he had visualised in his mind. They had travelled many miles through northern Malaya. He wanted to explore further, the towns of Penang and Alor Star. But they did not venture on. She was adamant it had to be Taiping because she loved the name. It meant 'eternal peace', a Chinese name for a Chinese family in search of a domicile.

'Papa was so encouraging,' she said.

'I can see how much he loved you,' I said.

'But he did not let me have my way when he told me that I was definitely going to an English school,' she said.

'Why did you want to go to Chinese school?' I asked.

'I spoke the language for one thing, and everything seemed much easier,' she replied.

We talked endlessly of the plans that grandfather had made for her education and of how fearful it was for her when she was encouraged to study at an English school and had to undertake an English curriculum. Geography was about all countries she had never visited. History consisted of some ancient history of the Egyptians. Lands and people totally alien to her was what she had to do endless hours of homework on. Literature which was entirely based on English literature, came as a final blow. She compared notes with some of her Chinese friends who were studying in a Chinese school. Their curriculum was based entirely on the Chinese Kuomintang system. She was totally envious of how much easier school was for them.

She had spent hours discussing differences between Eastern and Western thought with her father. They studied and debated the two systems of education. He told her why he had such strong convictions that leaving his homeland was the best resolution to all the problems they would have had to face if they had remained behind. They would carry with them in their hearts and minds, their culture of filial piety, which embedded qualities of harmony, loyalty, courtesy and honesty to family and nation. They would bring their traditions of family dinners and tea pouring. Love for one's country he once told her was like any love. Its core was not about possession, it was mostly about appreciation. In that way they would always have China in their hearts. Their culture belonged there and remained with them always. But in addition, an English education would give her the means to think for herself.

'My father cared so much about self-esteem and self-motivation,' she said seriously.

'Yes and I agree. Education encourages the search for new ideas, new questions and answers but individually, we need to believe and put much of that into practice,' I said emphatically.

'Otherwise we are simply robots,' she said.

'And machines do not do self-esteem,' I replied wisely.

'The school began with a piece of land of about three acres offered to the American missionaries for whom I worked,' she said totally changing the subject.

'Wow, that was amazingly generous of the Malayan government,' I replied.

'It was simply so exciting,' she said, 'I rushed back to tell my father.'

'What did he say?' I asked.

'"School",' she answered, 'just one word, "school".'

She was fascinating when she talked about the school she visualised. It was going to be a purpose-built school for 2000 students with ages ranging from six to thirteen; in other words, a big primary school. My mother had many requirements written down; properly ventilated classrooms, two gyms, a lunchroom adjacent to the tuck shop where school meals could be purchased at subsidised prices, washrooms with showers - the list went on.

She engaged a young but talented architect called Chen. He was from the capital city Kuala Lumpur, and worked together with an equally creative English partner, David. It was very exciting when the plans for the school were drawn out on architectural paper and stretched over the family dining table. My mother traced the ink lines with her fingers on the paper, as one would with a Leonardo da Vinci sketch, with a mixture of disbelief and full admiration.

In that way the building of the school was a 'family' affair. I remember her telling me that most of the important ideas were hatched out around the same dining table. Fundraising and listing out expenditure plans were the most intricate of all. My mother was often commended afterwards for how she raised every penny spent on that ambitious project. An initial endowment from her father was helpful, but the project took over four years to achieve funding completely. The money came mainly from donations from private companies, state government organisations and families.

My mother worked tirelessly at every fundraiser and pleaded and cajoled for money in every way she could. She had innovative ideas. A company of English soldiers built the road to the school because she had once helped the commanding colonel-in-chief with ideas for the procurement of local services of cooks for their kitchens. She had the same experiences from the workers from her father's plantations. These men also helped her with the landscaping of the school grounds, donating their services because she had helped their families with medical aid. It was an endless circle of asking for help where expertise could be given. I admired her fortitude, especially where it came to matters of the heart.

She fervently believed that her heart played an important role in her service. She had dreamt of giving the school to this town because she knew that an education to its young women would be a perpetual endowment. My brother and I were young recruits to her vision and we helped her whenever we were asked. We became especially good at creating and participating in fairs where there were stalls selling food or games for minute sums of money. However small, we were caught in that spiralling dream where we saw that little sums of money would finally add up to a big project completed. She would constantly remind us of this Chinese proverb;

'Be not afraid of growing slowly, be really afraid of standing still.'

The process from raising funds to building works took a long time because I remember traveling to England and finishing my first university degree. But I will never forget the first evening I returned home. My mother and I drove up to the club and the veranda where we had spent countless evenings drinking tea and discussing life. I knew from the way she acted that she had much more to tell me than I had to say to her. After all, what was there to say about a twenty-hour trip from right across the world? First, we talked about my grandfather, that really *beloved* of persons for her. He had died on his ninety-fourth birthday about a year before the school was completed. He had seen its skeletal shape and was in awe with its modern architectural form. From what I understood they had frequently spoken in riddles towards the end of his life. So much had changed between the old and the new, that he had found it difficult to grasp the hurried conversations about present day life.

'I am sure he was extremely proud of you,' I said with tears in my eyes.

'Yes, I mean he talked in Chinese proverbs I could hardly understand,' she said 'but I could see it in his eyes.'

'Bet he said something like,' I paused, 'not too badly done for a Mandarin's daughter.'

We laughed till we cried, again. It was a wonderful reunion.

Later we motored to the school. I could feel a blast of excitement envelope me. Then I saw it. The building looked incredible and almost in a supernatural environment. A modern structure among a beautiful natural landscape of tropical trees and plants. Beyond that my eyes fell on three immaculate playing fields.

They had positioned the school impeccably. For there was an undisturbed view somewhere between the classrooms and the offices, where an aspect of flame trees led to a brilliant vista of the peaks of the Maxwell Hills. I was left with my mother in our own deep but happy thoughts.

In China; from the Han dynasty, there were people who believed that an elixir for life longevity could be found on Yellow Mountain. We believed that where we stood, in a distant land and beneath some other peaks, my grandfather found his answer to that dream of prolonging his life's work. Through educating my mother and paving the way forward to her achievement of building that school; he probably must have realised that he had accomplished his mission. She did not become a sword-fighting woman warrior, but like most classical heroines in Chinese history she was loyal and courageous in helping the emperor achieve his vision for success

Lightning Source UK Ltd.
Milton Keynes UK
UKHW010001240922
409344UK00002B/156

9 781915 229250